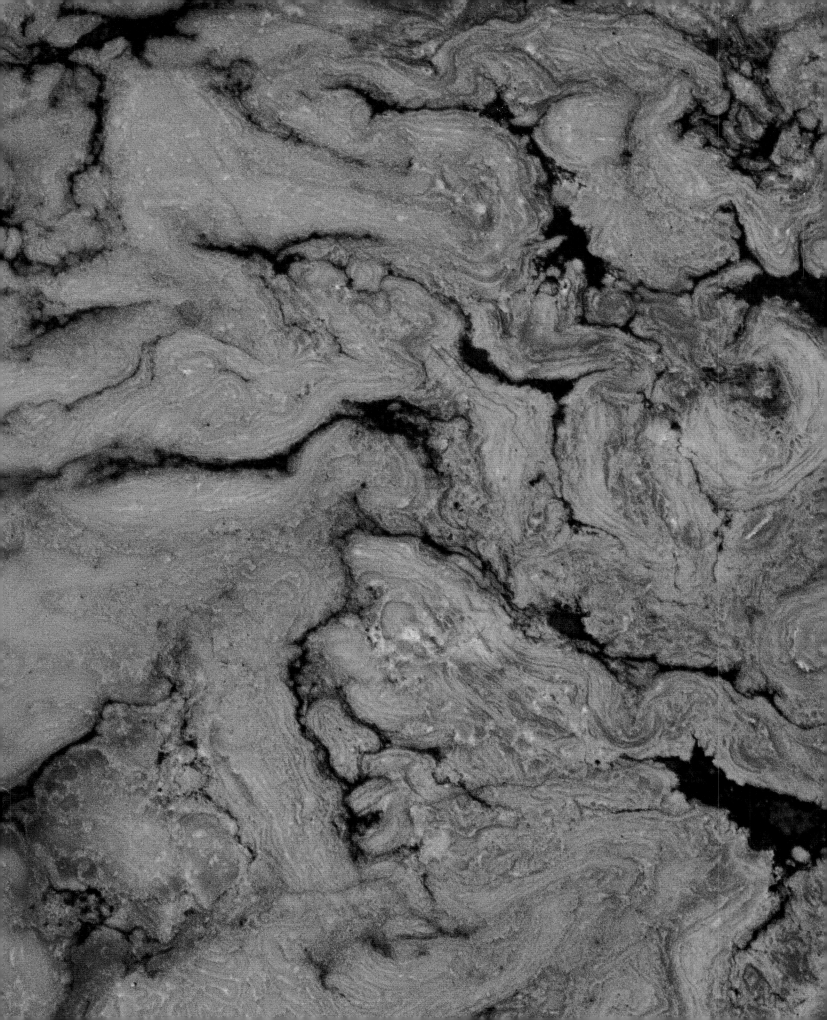

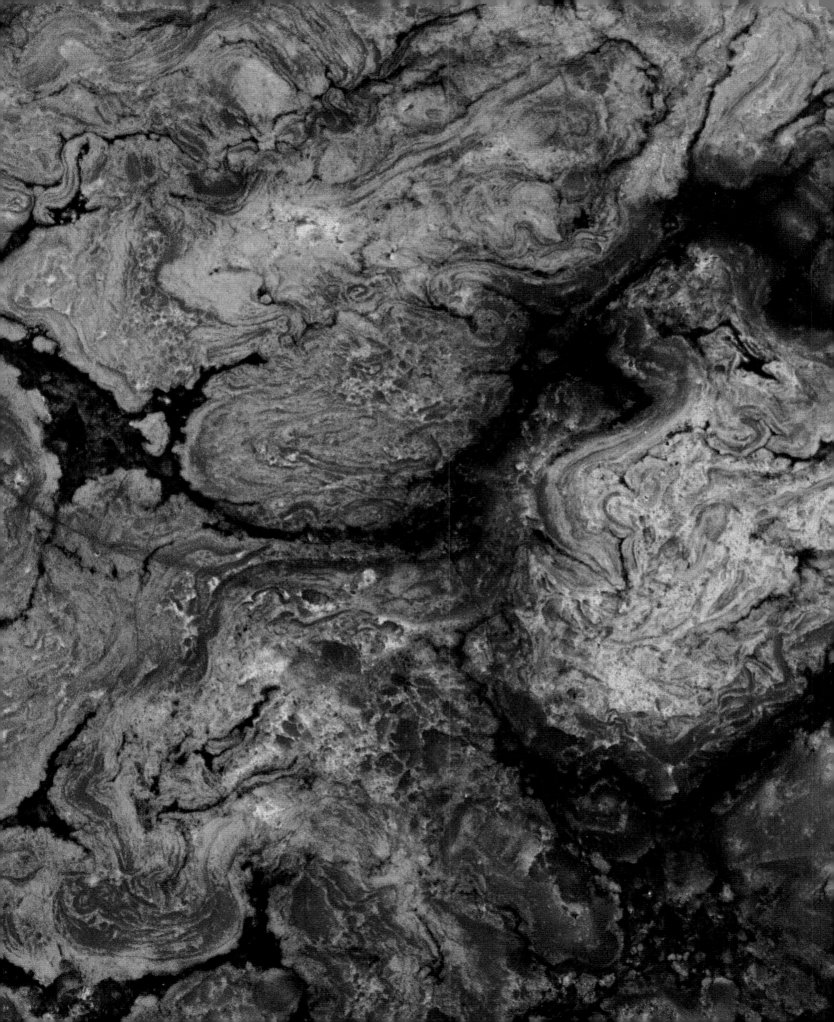

TEXT BY CAROL KARASIK   PHOTOGRAPHS BY JEFFREY JAY FOXX

HARRY N. ABRAMS, INC., PUBLISHERS

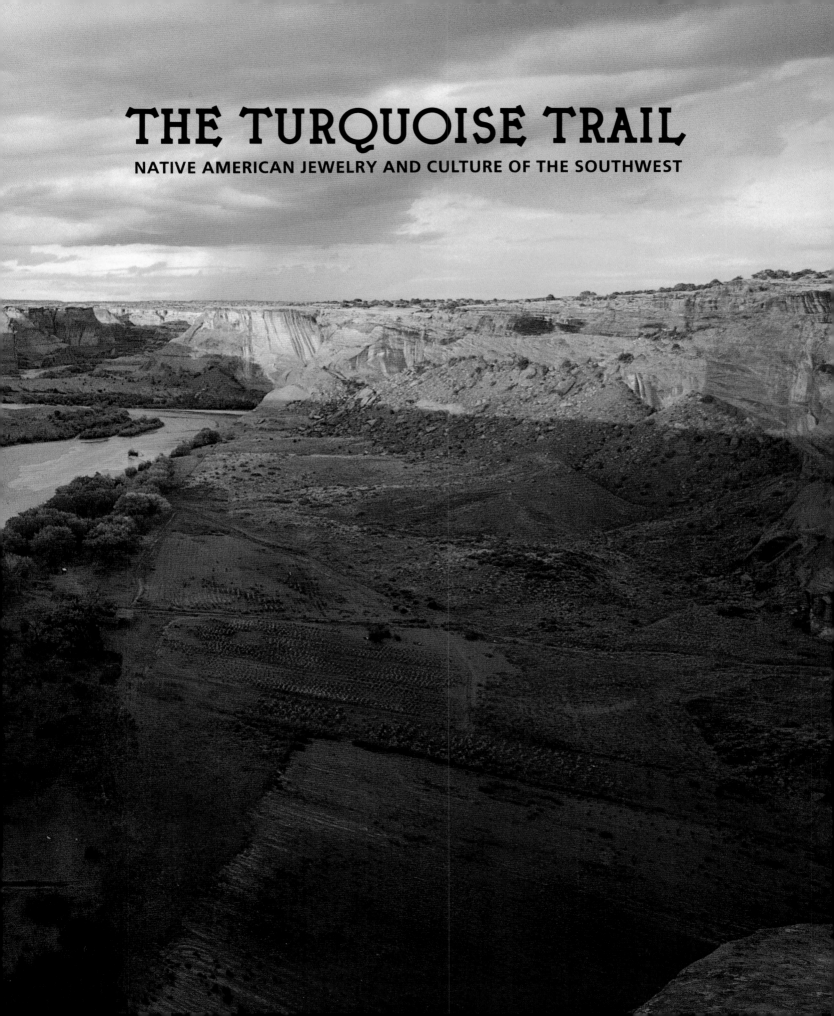

THE TURQUOISE TRAIL

NATIVE AMERICAN JEWELRY AND CULTURE OF THE SOUTHWEST

Editor: Beverly Fazio

Designers: Samuel N. Antupit and
Maria Miller

Map by Kristi Butterwick
Original drawings by Estela Hernández
Black-and-white photographs Courtesy
Museum of New Mexico. Negative numbers
are as follows: p. 14, 1413; p. 16, 36147;
p. 17, 12317; p. 19, 74527; p. 23, 144546;
p. 107, 16077; p. 108, 77474; p. 114, 16443;
p. 116, 37941; p. 117, 74870; p. 161, 40197;
p. 162, 89511; p. 164, 43501; p. 165, 57774;
p. 166, 38195; p. 167 above, 57017; p. 167
below, 15930; p. 209, 9189; p. 210, 72634;
p. 212, 16333; p. 215, 3895.

Library of Congress
Cataloging-in-Publication Data

Foxx, Jeffrey J. (Jeffrey Jay)
The turquoise trail : Native American
jewelry and culture of the Southwest /
photographs by Jeffrey Jay Foxx ; text by
Carol Karasik.
p.   cm.
Includes bibliographical references (p.   ).
ISBN 0-8109-3869-3
1. Indians of North America—Southwest,
New—Jewelry. 2. Turquoise. 3. Indians of
North America—Southwest, New—
Jewelry—Pictorial works. 4. Turquoise—
Pictorial works. 5. Indians of North
America—Southwest, New—Social life
and customs. 6. Indians of North America
—Southwest, New—Social life and
customs—Pictorial works. I. Karasik,
Carol. II. Title.
E78.S7F68   1993   93-20114
739.27'089'974079—dc20   CIP

Published in 1993 by Harry N. Abrams,
Incorporated, New York
A Times Mirror Company

Printed and bound in Japan

Page 1:
During their ancient migrations, Zuñis were led to a lake by the deer. Now deer, rain-birds, and flowers have a permanent place on water jars.

Pages 2–3:
Heart of the earth, heart of the sky, stone of sun, wind, rain, and fire. Turquoise, Sleeping Beauty Mine, Arizona.

Pages 4–5:
Canyon de Chelly cradled "the Ancient Ones," the Anasazis, whose cliff dwellings rang the canyon walls. Today Navajos summer along the river, lined with corn-fields and apple orchards.

Right:
Turquoise blooms on a squash blos-som necklace made for a young girl. Morenci turquoise, channel inlay, handwrought sil-ver beads. Zuñi, c. 1920. Artist unknown. Jeff Lewis' Trade Roots Collection, Ramah, New Mexico.

Overleaf:
Navajo drummer wears traditional turquoise and sil-ver *concha* belt and silver bow guard set with a single turquoise nugget. Gallup Intertribal Cere-monial, Gallup, New Mexico.

CONTENTS

Out in the desert, in the cycle of fire, ice, and light, the space is overpowering, beyond thought and imagination. I am saved by the strobes circling the state penitentiary twenty miles away, the dust kicked up by a pickup on Highway 14, the yellow toy train passing slowly across the endless yellow plain. In the face of oblivion you learn to scan the horizon for details, know the ground beneath your feet.

From my front porch I look out across a dry sea to a wide gash high on Turquoise Mountain. Some days the dynamite blasts from the gold mine shake the seabed and rattle the glass. It rattles me, those company men with their bulldozers scraping out the last of the gold. Even in moonlight I can see that white scar on the shoulder of the mountain, bare and cold. West of the gold works is the mouth of a mine leading down to blue seams I cannot see, even in sunlight. When the mountain rides through storm clouds and rain, it stands for all things precious and invisible. Piercing the Southwestern sky are mountains so black in mystery, so luminous in power, they are obvious dwelling places of thunder and the gods. Chalchihuitl, Turquoise Mountain, holds the sky inside its blue core.

Every mountain tells a story. Riches buried in the earth are the stuff of myths and revery. In the dreamscape of the American West, the search for gold, lost mines, and buried treasure is the dominant theme of legend and recorded history. Always they are tales of self-discovery and high adventure. Always they reveal some truth greater than earthly treasure. Always there is a price.

Turquoise is synonymous with the landscape and peoples of the Southwest. In streets, plazas, shopping malls, and in the middle of the desert; over plain dresses, velvet blouses, satin skirts, cowboy shirts, and ceremonial costumes, the Pueblo and Navajo Indians wear turquoise necklaces, turquoise pendants, turquoise bracelets, belts, and brooches with exquisite unconcern. Elsewhere, turquoise jewelry may come and go with fashion. Here turquoise is more precious than gold, an enduring expression of Native American culture.

Turquoise has been prized for thousands of years. The Cerrillos mines on Turquoise Mountain are the oldest known source of turquoise in the Southwest. The mountain's rich deposits were mined by the Tano Indians of Kunyaonweji, the "Turquoise Pueblo." In workshops at Chaco Canyon, New Mexico, artisans polished stones that were coveted by nobles of distant lands. Legend has it that the rare blue and green turquoise from Mount Chalchihuitl was traded as far as Oaxaca, Mexico. The royal crowns of the Mixtec kings were adorned with turquoise from Cerrillos. Montezuma II, last emperor of the Aztecs, wore pendants of Cerrillos turquoise as amulets of good fortune and

Merchant with staff and backpack, Mimbres

long life. The turquoise trade flowed from the heart of New Mexico to California and Arkansas. In Mexico, trade followed the routes of the Toltecs, Tarascans, and Aztecs and the older Teotihuacán, Maya, and Olmec civilizations. In exchange for turquoise, Mexican merchants supplied the Anasazi and Hohokam people of the Southwest with macaw feathers, copper bells, and obsidian. The cultural affluence of Chaco Canyon, whose architecture and elaborate road systems were the most sophisticated in Pre-Columbian North America, rested on the lucrative turquoise trade. Along with commerce in ceremonial objects, merchants exchanged information, stories, and beliefs. Trade, which united religion with commerce, bound the peoples of Mesoamerica and the Southwest into one vast cultural sphere.

Turquoise, once a luxury intended solely for the nobility, is worn by every native of the Southwest as a sign of relative wealth. The rain gods, the kachinas, wear it. The earth mother herself was once a little figure made of turquoise, before Talking God brought Changing Woman to life.

If you believe, as Native Americans believe, that the earth is alive, then all things, no matter how small or apparently inanimate, are precious. In the modern age, there is still this primal recognition of life-giving rock: the smooth stones that lie in streams, the clear quartz that juts from limestone,

the humble stone, found on a walk in the woods, the little black pebble lying mysteriously on the path to your door. The crystal in which you see the rainbow, the crystal ball in which gypsies see the future. There are stones medicine men keep in their sacred bundles because they possess powers of healing. There are gemstones set in royal crowns that control the destiny of empires, the Blarney Stone that grants the gift of gab, the philosopher's stone that transforms base metals into gold. There is the stone that comes to you in dreams and the magic ring you wear on your finger.

The presence of sky and water inside a stone is miraculous, a piece of heaven on earth, a round ripple of water inside the hard dry pebble. In the mineral world, a geologist will tell you, these elements do intermingle. The sky comes down to earth and enters stone. Oxygen mixes with andesite, augite, feldspar, kaolin clay, aluminum, and traces of copper. In time, turquoise grains and crystals grow. The stone holds moisture. If turquoise dries out in sunlight, it will even change color, from bright blue to leaf green. The elements found in turquoise are present in seaweed, hay, eggs, and feathers.

No one knows who first noticed a clear blue line running through gray rock, or who first struck the surface and saw sky and water flow. But from that time forth, turquoise was cherished above all else in creation—turquoise, stone of sky, stone of water, stone of blessings, good fortune, and long life in the parched infinity of mountains, red rock, and sand.

The relationship between stones and human culture is, like all relationships in nature, mysterious, impenetrable. Stone Age hunters and gatherers of the Southwest lived a nomadic existence, setting up temporary camps where animals and plants were plentiful. Sometimes they were lured to travel in search of stones that produced pretty pigments, better spearpoints, or fine pendants. Archaeologists tend to describe Paleoindian life in terms of raw necessity. But as the Hopis say, there is more to life than corn. Their ancestors may have lingered in one place because they had discovered there, besides a source of food and water, something of beauty, a source of turquoise or red ochre. Or perhaps they beheld a spirit in the rocks that urged them to adapt rather than move on. Out of the rock, the Pueblos say, they were born.

Related tribes continued south, into Mexico and Central America. They domesticated corn; erected cities and pyramids of stone; developed astronomy, mathematics, art, and a written literature; and managed complex systems of government and trade. Commodities from the kingdoms of Mexico were transfered to their Hohokam, Mogollon, and Anasazi cousins in the north. Turquoise was shipped south. Philosophical and religious ideas were exchanged. People were willing to travel over harsh terrains, sometimes for years, to obtain objects of elemental beauty. They did not always speak the same language. They did not necessarily like one another. Their nations were sometimes at war. Yet for years there was active communication among distant and distinct peoples along well-traveled trade routes, economic interdependence, and spiritual affinities. *The Turquoise Trail* describes the New World before Europeans arrived, when no artificial national border divided the cultural area of Mesoamerica.

The Spanish were lured to the Americas by visions of gold. In pursuit of that vain dream, they attempted to erase or exploit every aspect of New World culture. When they learned of the riches of Mount Chalchihuitl, the Spaniards immediately seized the mines and enslaved the Tano Indians.

Gold was discovered in Mount Chalchihuitl three centuries later. The historic Turquoise Trail ran from Cedar Crest to Golden, boom towns during the gold rush of the 1870s, ghost towns now, along a road that once led south into Mexico.

In the last hundred years, archaeologists have been mining America's past, bringing to light the long traditions of surviving cultures in the Southwest and Mexico. Knowledge of Pre-Columbian America also is based on the journals of Spanish explorers and priests, who present eyewitness accounts of the life and customs of Native American cultures at the time of the Conquest. Those documents, colored by the illusions and biases of the chroniclers, reveal as much about the European mind in its first dramatic encounter with the alien peoples of the New World. Added to the enormous body of scientific, historic, and oral literature is the photographic record produced by nineteenth-century itinerant photographers, who explored the West and captured its landscape and peoples permanently on film.

When ranchers first discovered the ruins of the Southwest, they attributed them to Aztecs fleeing

Mexico at the time of the Conquest. So, we find names like Aztec for ancient sites in New Mexico. Since the turn of the century the evidence for contact has grown and the story infinitely richer.

For Native Americans of the Southwest, relations with their southern brothers are still alive. Medicine men continue to make religious pilgrimages to West Coast Mexico in search of herbs and peyote (a major issue in the courts). The Hopis and Zuñis continue to depend on traders for supplies of parrot feathers. And silversmiths continue to acknowledge their debt to the itinerant craftsmen from Mexico who introduced jewelry-making to the Southwest over one hundred years ago.

The jeweler's art encapsulates the past and present. The symbols stamped on bracelets and *concha* belts, the designs of bowguards and squash blossom necklaces emanate from ancient beliefs. In turquoise and silver is written a long and still living history.

Santa Fé was the northernmost outpost of the Camino Real, the Royal Road, which supplanted the Turquoise Trail during the Spanish colonial era. When I arrived at the southern end of the Camino Real, in San Cristóbal de Las Casas, Chiapas, I saw the future. The colonial city is a busy market and tourist center, with 150,000 Maya Indians living in the surrounding mountains. The nearby Lacandon rainforest, which had been a source of exotic feath-ers for the early Pueblo tribes, is threatened by deforestation, oil drilling, and hydroelectric dams. At both ends of the Camino Real, at both ends of the Turquoise Trail, a people had been vanquished and had risen again. Distantly related, the Pueblos and the Maya are traditional peoples who have withstood the most dire periods of cultural transition. May they remain as permanent as the stone at the heart of sky and water.

NOTE TO THE READER

The Aztec word *chalchihuitl*, scholars agree, most often means ordinary green jade. But sometimes the ancients used the same word to describe turquoise. A color blindness—the inability to distinguish blue from green—is prevalent throughout the New World; thus, most native languages have a single word for blue and green. The problem is compounded by inexpert observers who cannot tell one gemstone from another. And so, the Spaniards confused fine jade with emeralds; or confused green turquoise, and blue, with malachite, serpentine, jasper, and chrysoprase. Mountains named for the gems they contained suffered the same fate. Turquoise had to wait for the Turks to name it, and by then it was too late.

MESOAMERICA

N

- ⛰ ARCHAEOLOGICAL SITE
- ⌂ PUEBLO
- ✹ MODERN CITY
- ⚒ TURQUOISE MINE

KILOMETERS
0   500
MILES
0   300

AMERICAN SOUTHWEST

Sangre de Cristo Mts.
Mesa Verde
HOPI   NAVAJO
Salmon   Aztec
Cañon de Chelly
San Juan   Folsom
Chaco Canyon   San Ildefonso
Santo Domingo   Santa Fe
Zuni   Pecos
Phoenix   Acoma   Cerrillos
Snaketown   Abo
Salt River
Gila R.
Casa Grande
Hachita
Rio Grande

Sonora River
Casas Grandes
Yaqui R.
Copper Canyon
Batopilas

Guasave
Aztatlán

MEXICO

Sierra Madre Occidental

Sombrerete
Alta Vista
Zacatecas
La Quemada

Compostela
Ixtlan del Rio
Guadalajara
Teuchtitlan
Culiacan   Queretero
Lake Chapala
Tlatilco   Tula
Lake Patzcuaro   Mexico City   Teotihuacan
Colima   Colhuacan
Tzintzuntzan   Tenochtitlan   Lake Texcoco
Malinalco   Chalcatzingo   Tehuacan Valley

Monte Alban
Oaxaca
Isthmus of Tehuantepec
La Venta
Palenque
Chiapa de Corzo
San Cristobal   Yaxchilan   Uaxactun
  Tikal
Izapa
Kaminaljuyu
Motagua   Copan

Chichen Itza
Cozumel
Cobá

Gulf of Mexico

Pacific Ocean

BELIZE

GUATEMALA   HONDURAS

K BUTTERWICK
1993

Portrait of a Zuñi chieftain wearing hishi strands and shell pendant, c. 1900. Photograph by J. R. Willis.

CHAPTER 1

STONE OF SKY

...whoever lives out there in space must surely call Earth "the blue planet"...

—Astronaut Ed White
Apollo 12 Space Expedition

The badlands north of Santa Fé are the color of bleached bones. The sandstone is a giant fossil pocked with a million holes where men, women, and animals once made homes along slow streams. Dunes and arroyos lie in a dry half sleep, a burnt-out, blank yellow vision of the future, of some exhausted planet, our own, gone dead.

Across the Rio Grande rise the pink cliffs of the Pajarito Plateau. One of the geologic wonders of the world, it is a table, a fan, and a mile-high maze of canyons, a cold volcanic extravagance. Now cattle graze on locoweed inside the extinct green cauldron.

The plateau is named for the little birds that dart among dry chamisa, scattered ranch houses, Baptist churches, and gray barracks left over from World War II. Dirt roads wind past Ponderosa pine, burnt forest, and barbed wire. Riveted to the edge of the cliffs squat the storm huts of Los Alamos National Laboratory, home of the atom bomb. The research stations are off-limits, silver shrines of aluminum siding, Biblical in power. Perched up there with the little birds, the Lost Alamites are listening for messages from outer space and measuring the annual fall of nutrinos on the green grass. A thousand years ago, and a stone's throw away, the Anasazi Indians were living like swallows in the cliffs.

A fine atomic dust seems to have settled on the land below, its silence scored by 60 million years of magnificent catastrophe. Under the mountains, feldspars and phosphates wed, troves of turquoise, silver, and gold are shining. Inside this immense reliquary, fantastic creatures laid down their bones before the waters of the Rio Grande flowed and the Sangre de Cristo range exploded from the Rockies.

Digging into this convoluted geologic wonder, paleontologists found skulls of the saber-toothed tiger. Over the river and up the canyon two men, to their utter amazement, uncovered the colossal shinbone of a dinosaur so huge it staggers the mind. The shin, when propped on its incredible, trampoline-sized tip, stands two stories high. Scientists were speechless. The usual classifications were too mild to encompass a monster that had been stalking people's dreams through one hundred thousand black nights. In a deep bow to popular imagination, they call the awesome creature Supersaur.

This recent discovery changes the picture completely. In the days when those gigantic lizards roamed freely, they must have rearranged the open spaces. They would lumber down from Taos in three giant steps and volcanoes quaked. Whole ecosys-

tems were stamped out by their thundering feet. Local experts figure a flying monster frightened them near Provo, Utah, and started a stampede that formed the San Juan Basin and the Rio Grande Gorge. The silt from their enormous tread raised the foothills of the Sangre de Cristo and Jemez Mountains. Quiet creatures, they chomped on giant ferns, waded in the sunless swamp that this arid land once was, mindless of the havoc they had wrought. And then, for no reason, they were pelted by meteors from outer space, the earth was buried in darkness, and the dinosaurs were erased. The saber-toothed tiger and mammoth, no match for those monsters in size or strength, roared through this valley long after.

Here, trailing bands of Stone Age hunters drifted down from the Colorado glaciers. Here, Anasazi farmers, having abandoned their towns at Chaco Canyon, carved shelters in the tufa ridges and portraits of gods on the canyon walls. Here, a nineteenth-century ethnographer, Adolph Bandelier, discovered thousands of cliff dwellings up the canyons and concluded that they had been built by the ancestors of the Pueblos. Defying the thought of his day, Bandelier was the first European to corroborate the Pueblo version of history, that this land of geologic time and primordial beasts was the home of an ancient race of people. He called the "Ancient Ones" the Delight Makers.

In Frijoles Canyon lie the ruins of Tyuonyi, an Anasazi village abandoned centuries ago and washed by the same slow winds eroding the ridge. Cliff dwellings open like nests, row upon row. High above the aspen is a natural rock shelter, and a thousand handholds chipped into the wind. Below, the cellular rooms and empty plaza, sleeping in the curve of the long, green-shadowed river, sink as if they drifted underwater. A low sea tone sounds from the boulders. Five ladders, nailed to the cliff, reach up to the ledge.

Inside the stone mouth is a ladder descending into night. Halfway between earth and heaven circles the twilight of the kiva. Cut into the stone floor, a black hole leads deeper into darkness, deep into the heart of the underworld. Round that hole men had danced and prayed. They came into this world climbing, and so they made a ceremony of climbing: a sheer ascent to the cave in air and a round dance in the dark stone, under the round sun, the round moon, the new moon, night.

Along the rim of the canyon walls runs a ribbon of white stone. This thin white streak marks the brief span of humankind on earth. Resting in this silence, staring into the shadow of the sun, the marvellous dark of a billion years coming on from behind, one can see, as if through a sudden opening in the rock, all time, the minute brevity of our passing, the clear light of this and all worlds.

Long before the world was, the people dwelled in a cave deep below the surface of the earth. The spirits were dwelling there, too. The people were not human then. They lived like ants, always toiling, always stumbling about in the restless dark with their flickering antennae. Then Spider Woman came. "I will give you new life," she said. "I will weave a long thread of silk. I will set down this skein in the darkness."

One by one, the ancestors climbed through darkness, and as they climbed they changed their skins, they shed their slippery wings, scales, and shells. Who knows how long it took or how many levels of the earth. They passed through many worlds.

Above them a light that was neither sun nor shadow broke through a hole in the stone. Some were blinded and fell far below. Their new eyes weren't used to it. Some dropped off because the strain was too great. All the gods and spirits stayed behind.

Turquoise Boy, the Navajos say, was leading the way for the rest. He was the first to step on the land. Immediately he sank up to his knees in mud, because the earth wasn't ready. When it dried out a bit he walked north, south, east, and west. He established the world quarters and he named their colors. He established the four sacred mountains at the corners of the horizon. He established the center below Great Mountain, which is invisible because it is too big to see. When the world was ready, the ancestors walked upon the surface of the land. "We shall stand erect as men and women," were the first words they would say.

The Hopis emerged through a blow hole at the bottom of the Grand Canyon. The Zuñis, after painful passage from womb-world to womb-world to womb-world inside the Earth Mother, swam out through a salt lake near the Little Colorado River. The Navajos appeared at the foot of Black Mountain. All endured the darkness, the slow metamorphosis through successive stages of animal life. All suffered as they groped through the weirdness of the lower worlds toward a final blinding birth from rock.

Antelope Priest emerges from an underground kiva. Photographed during Hopi Snake Dance, c. 1900.

This epic journey was the triumphant beginning of the long and beautiful journey over the road of life. After their appearance on the land, the ancestors, with powerful hearts, continued their courageous wanderings. But there was not enough light. First Man took a huge piece of turquoise, shaped it into a round disc, and hung it in the sky. The new sun lit the way toward their destined homes on the brown steppes, the black mesas, the broad forests of red stone.

The gods refused to let the Hopis rest. After crossing four steppingstones in the western sea, clans traveled east to the Atlantic, west again to the Pacific, south into the land of the red snake, and north to the land of ice at the rim of the world. Their footsteps made a giant cross over the Americas before they turned, turned home. They carried their insignias and signs, their clan symbols, and sacred books of prophesy. The Badger Clan and the Bear Clan were the first to arrive, and they wept. The Snake Society and the Antelope Society vowed they would share their powers and dance together. The Parrot Clan vowed to stay. And all the clans made peace and prayed and promised to serve as guardians for the whole earth for all time.

The ancestors, paleoarchaeologists speculate, crossed from Siberia and northern Japan over the Bering Strait 30,000 years ago. Brave fisherfolk

Clown with horned serpent mask,
Mimbres

paddled skin boats along the frozen shorelines, hugging the glacial coasts until they could put in safely at warm, ice-free harbors as far south as Peru. Hunters trudged under heavy furs across the ice sheets, year after year, following herds of mammoth. They plodded up the Yukon and Mackenzie Rivers, over towering mountain passes, and down the ice-free ribbon of grass that ran along the eastern flanks of the Rockies and on to the Great Plains.

They carried with them stone hunting weapons. They brought with them the words for *spirit, stone, water*, and *breath*. They carried stories of the red dragon of the earth and the blue dragon of the sky. The shamans knew the languages of the animals, the calls of birds, and the voices of the butterfly. They knew the wild herbs, which also grew on the vast Siberian steppes, that cured the sick of pains and witchcraft. They knew the healing powers of quartz and agate, the jaspers that brought thunder. In trances shamans traveled to other worlds of snow and crystal, worlds beneath the sea, beyond the stars. An animal soul was living inside the human body, the truest friend, the shamans said. At night the companion soul would wander, and the dreamer would see the forests, plains, and waters through the eyes of antelope, wolf, otter, eagle, mountain lion, or bear. The people sang to appease the souls of the beasts they slew. They lived and

died in the open and their bones were borne away by the birds.

On they journeyed, and after 150 generations of walking, the First Americans crossed the continents for which they had no name and reached the tip of South America. There they stared once more on the hard white sea and ceased their tireless exploration.

The discovery of the New World—pieced together from bits of bone, grinding stones, and spearpoints left at ancient campsites in Alaska, Florida, and New Mexico, in dry caves in the Tehuacan Valley of Mexico, Costa Rica, and Ecuador, by fires on the icy shores of Tierra del Fuego—was the first of the Long Walks in the history of the first people of this land.

The scientific version of the migration story, unlike Hopi oral history, is less than one hundred years old, and changing daily. Scholars of the early nineteenth century had a shorter timeframe. They imagined that the Indians were cast into the Paradise of the New World a decade or so before the Pilgrims landed. The earth, they reckoned by the Bible, was created in 4004 B.C. For years American settlers had been puzzled by the mysterious man-made hills that loomed in pastures from West Virginia to Georgia, amazed by the snake mounds coiled among the trees of Ohio. And what giant race of men had raised enormous pyramids in the remote jungles of Mexico? Since Indians were considered incapable of such feats, many scholars concluded that the astonishing ruins had been the work of unsung European voyagers. Digging deeper into history, pedants, priests, painters, and counts staked their fortunes and their lives trying to prove that the lost civilizations of the New World had been ruled by Phoenicians, by the Lost Tribes of Israel, by Madoc, High King of Wales. When Thomas Jefferson excavated a hill near his home in Charlottesville, Virginia, he suspected that the elaborate burial mound was the work of American Indians who had occupied the land centuries before the white man came. Establishing the great Age of Man in America, and the true origins of New

The melancholy air of the Flute Ceremony drifts over the spring, a song of migration and emergence to the fourth world, led by the Hopi flute-playing deity Kokopelli. Mishongnovi Pueblo. Photograph by Frederick Monsen, 1907.

World cultures, has been an extraordinary adventure in itself.

George McJunkin used the science of the eye. He was a buffalo hunter, ox driver, bronco rider, cow puncher, and the best roper in the country. He was foreman of the Crowfoot Ranch, ten miles outside Folsom, New Mexico. He was the son of slaves, and when he was freed at the end of the Civil War he taught himself to write. He knew more about birds than anyone within five hundred miles of Denver. He had been a rockhound since he was a boy. He spent his nights reading. He spent his days scrutinizing the wind. He was a free man in the saddle, accustomed to the long march of time.

On a clear autumn afternoon in 1908, McJunkin was riding along the south fork of Wild Horse Arroyo, when he saw a white protrusion at the bottom of the gulch. He took out a pair of barbed-wire clippers and began to dig bones. The man knew everything there was to know about cattle. He had crossed the Staked Plains and had seen thousands of buffalo carcasses rotting in the landscape. He knew these bones belonged to something older and bigger.

One day he happened to mention his discovery to the local blacksmith, Carl Scwachneim. Seven years later, George and Carl set out for the arroyo in the company of a bank teller, a priest, a brick-layer from Lebanon, and an amateur taxidermist. All were impressed by the size of the bones. In 1925 Carl wrote to the Denver Museum to notify them of the find. Dr. Jesse Figgins, physical anthropologist and director of the museum, came to Folsom the following year. Immediately Figgins recognized that the bones belonged to an extinct bison (*Bison antiquus figginsi*). The men dug further. Eight feet below the surface, directly under a live oak tree, lay the complete twelve-thousand-year-old skeleton of a bison. Inside the cavity of the body, near the base of the fifth vertebra, Carl found a broken spearpoint, two inches long and beautifully crafted of amber-colored agate. Later he found another point made of jasper. It was July 14, 1926.

The Folsom points were the first artifacts found in direct association with an extinct animal, indisputable evidence that man had been in America for at least twelve thousand years. Furthermore, the points were superbly made. The artisans who had manufactured the weapons had achieved a level of craftsmanship unmatched in the Old World. The Folsom points were the most important finds in the history of American archaeology.

There have been countless serendipitous discoveries since. During excavations near Clovis, New Mexico, in a blue clay bog at the edge of the Staked Plains, a bulldozer made the work go faster. The driver shifted gears too fast. The rock caved in like

Deer-fish, Mimbres

glass. And down the crenelated tunnel roared a river of bones: mammoth, mastodon, camels, horses. The pollen count in the area showed enough vegetal support for 100,000 bison. Plenty to eat for a large nomadic family and plenty of pony breast, camel rump, and mammoth toes to keep on ice for a hundred winters.

Paleoarchaeologists are hunting everywhere, living the lives of Paleoindians. They are knee-deep in Bluebird Creek, which is wider than some rivers. They are wading in icy run-offs meandering down the moraines: tip of the glacier's big toe and still wiggling. They are digging down into something near creation: digging through layers so riddled with Tertiary Intrusives it may be impossible to date anything they find, digging in ground that has been shifting since gold soared in the 1960s and the miners came out to hose down the banks. The miners are looking for gold and washing away the tracks, and the bone hunters are looking for Adam, Eve, and old Aunt Nelly.

They are walking the summits of the Rockies, plotting trails across the high frozen passes. They are out on the burning desert, roaming dead river-beds for flints, half-delirious, trying to scratch time with a dental pick. The world moves in slow motion. They are shuffling through the carboniferous ferns and lycopodium, snoozing under the late mesozoic trees, minds sluggish as Cucharas clay.

Years have been spent scrambling over rocks, hanging on ledges, crawling through guano and sloth dung in high desert caves. Months have been spent in pitch black, following subterranean rivers until the rowers were at one with the dead. The occupational hazards, the failure of returning home empty-handed, are akin to the risks encountered by Stone Age men. The job demands the kind of empathy a hunter feels for the hunted, a psyche that cuts through time to one's distant brother. There is the same terrible futility in spending a lifetime seeking out the smallest particle to add to the heap, and the same common wonder in seeing the destiny of humankind in one agate flake, one unifacial Clovis point, one sinolongate backshovel incisor.

After all we've unscrambled, botched, found, lost, found, and glued together, we've made no definite headway since 1926 in pushing back man's occupation of this continent. If you want to go back to the source, you may have to enter the land at a place like Folsom. You will have to brave the elements on Johnson Mesa. There you will gaze across the Palisades toward the snow-capped San Juan Mountains. Beside the raw power of nature in all its beauty and breadth, the Folsom site is so inconspicuous only someone like George McJunkin who knew the treeless terrain by heart could have noticed something different.

You feel a certain awe standing there in the red mud, out of reach of the fifty-mile-an-hour winds. Winter nights, snow buries the roads and you pray you make it over the bluff and home before the wind changes. Now junipers are creaking and pale chamisa is coming to life after the long eight-month winter. Steers are chewing sage and sparse yellow grass under the double cones of Capitan Peak. Telephone wires are chirping like sparrows. Horns snag on the barbed-wire fences.

You feel a pang of melancholy for the old ones and for the little girls skipping rope in front of the museum. You feel a link with the survivors of the flood. You shiver for all the lone riders and for George McJunkin, a black cowboy, on his way home one Sunday afternoon, dreaming about a cup of tea, thinking of the devastation wrought by the Cimarron River, when whiteness caught his eye and he stumbled upon the signs of an earlier human presence.

In the age of stone, people made the rocks their mirrors. Sandstone columns were the heroes and maidens of their stories. The mirage stone held their illusions. Quartz held their dreams. The bloodstone was their blood and fire. Crystals rescued the souls of the sick. The stone of the moon drove them mad. The stone of the sun was their map. Grains of mica lit the stars. Azurite was the night. When they heard tales about the sea they saw it as a changing lake of quicksilver. When men spoke of love they felt a burning stone in the heart. When they spoke of sorrow they said it weighed like a lodestone. The earth was a stone, shaped like a diamond, lying flat on the back of a turtle who slept like a stone in the sea.

Spearpoints contained their creative spirit, which flew to the hearts of animals. Some express a human purpose too refined for ordinary hunting. The points were made to speed through time and signal the supernatural, the divine. For these, a special pilgrimage was required, in search of a stone of rare grain, color, and hardness. A band living near Drake, in western Colorado, sent members south to Texas to secure a perfect slab of green alibates stone. For months craftsmen flaked and honed until the fluted points took the shape of long thin leaves. The most beautiful were buried in human ashes, and the soul carried them down through stone passages and into the land of the dead.

The earliest peoples possessed a powerful urge to transcend the immediate, to cross great distances in search of precious stones, and to fashion the most basic utilitarian tool into an object that would serve the immortal soul eternally. The impulse was religious, the weapon spiritual, and the transforming force the work of art.

Life granted them enough leisure time to incise designs on ivory tusks or polish round bone beads. Traders traveled to and from the coasts of California and Texas bringing shells to be worn as pendants, shells to be strung as necklaces and anklets, shells that let the desert people hear the sound of the sea. For ceremonies they had shells that trumpeted, shells that rattled, and dancing drums of turtle shell to beat with a carved antler.

The bands who roamed the Southwest were part of a second great wave of immigrants who crossed the Bering Strait and eventually settled the land from Oregon to Central America. They spoke related languages and they shared a similar way of life. When the climate shifted around 7000 B.C.,

Yacatecutli, god of merchants,
Teotihuacán

changing the lakes, marshes, and inland seas to wide basins of grass, they adjusted to an arid environment that showed little promise. They learned how to survive without water.

Eternally inventive, adaptable, and busy, women gathered wild grains, fruits, and berries, stitched hides, beat bark, plaited cloth, braided sandals of yucca. They strung together shells, bones, stones, and feathers to wear around their necks and weave through their hair. The women used stones to grind nuts and taught the men how to flake spearpoints, darts, and arrows. Twice a month the men went hunting. As the great herds of bison and mammoth died out, people increasingly relied on the wild plants the women gathered. Soon the women learned to make baskets so tight they could hold water. Yellow were their baskets, yellow were their stones, yellow would be their seed.

What tales they must have told in the afterglow. From the ashes of a thousand night fires rose a long, winding story, woven with gossip of the day's events, the experiences of the old, and many exaggerated adventures. The saga was rooted in the wisdom of the caves, in the cycles of the earth and seasons, and in the human body. In time the storyteller would be buried with her belongings, a turquoise bead placed in her mouth so she would retain the power of speech in the next world. History would be an elaborate variation of the story.

One day two women were searching for piñon nuts and juniper berries, when they saw a flock of ravens sitting in a tree. The birds had something strange and yellow in their beaks. Naturally the women were curious. They crept closer.

"What's that you're eating?" one of the women asked. "It looks very tasty. Can't you see we're starving."

"Try some," said the ravens.

The woman bit into the yellow stalk. It was the size of her baby finger. She almost broke her tooth on the tiny seeds. But they tasted good and sweet.

"Where did you find this? Don't you have any more?" the women asked.

"We found it far to the south," laughed the ravens as they flew off. Perhaps they took pity on the poor starving women. They circled in a great black cloud, and one by one little yellow seeds descended from the sky.

As luck would have it, the very next day the rains came. Soon the seeds sprouted and small green shoots sprang up in a lazy patch under the trees. In fall, when the chamisa was in full bloom, the maize was sweet enough to eat. The women gathered the grain in baskets and carried it home to their cave. Everyone had enough corn to eat.

The trouble was, there was nothing left. And so two people were sent to the south in search of the grass that bore sweet kernels inside green husks with hairy tassels.

Just as they were starting out, a man from the south appeared, bearing in his tumpline hundreds of ears of dried corn. He told the people how to plant and care for it. He told them it would change their lives. In exchange they gave him a string of shells and five blue beads. They promised him a permanent place in their songs. The stranger was content.

From Guatemala to the Pacific Northwest, Indian tribes say that a raven gave the gift of corn to man. The Hopi believe that corn was brought from the south by the great god Quetzalcoatl, the Feathered Serpent, in the guise of a raven. Some say the raven found the corn in a cave.

Portrait of a young dancer, Ohwo-wo-Songwi of San Ildefonso Pueblo, in traditional tablita headdress with symbol of crescent moon. Photograph by Edward S. Curtis, 1905.

Among scientists the origin of corn remains a vital question—as penetrating and nagging as weeds—because agriculture is the essence of civilization. Plant geneticists guess that modern corn probably evolved from various hybrids of wild maize, which spread by pollen blowing in the wind. Given sharp eyes, the hunter-gatherers surely noted that birds were fond of gathering it in their beaks. But where was the source?

Central Mexico may be one beginning, the Fertile Crescent of the New World. After a twenty-year search, archeologist Richard S. McNeish found a wild charred corn cob, the size of a black bean, buried in the ashes of an ancient hearth. The hearth was deep inside Coxcatlan Cave in the Tehuacan Valley. The little cobs were eight thousand years old and perfectly preserved.

For millennia people were happily gathering wild cobs, until some clever woman discovered that the food tossed in the midden heap had sprouted. Tribes living in Central Mexico already were growing squash, bottle gourds, and chilis; they added maize to the list of plants that needed tending. By 3000 B.C. they were clearing hard ground, planting, hoeing, weeding, and praying for rain.

The plants flourished because they had little competition from other wild plants struggling for life in the arid soil. After centuries of selecting the best kernels and crossbreeding the most desirable plants, Indians developed hundreds of varieties of corn, as many as scientists have engineered today and perhaps even more suited to deserts, mountains, swamps, and rainforests: remarkably diverse climates and terrains that remarkably diverse groups of men and women chose to call their homeland.

Following the path laid down in the great myth of emergence, the Mogollon, Hohokam, and Anasazi tribes of the Southwest literally had risen out of the caves and onto the surface of the earth. Some chose the canyon floor and narrow river valleys, and others scaled the tops of broad mesas. When they found true center, they built hives of rooms around the plaza and around the kiva, where they came together at the gateway to another world. The fields on which their lives depended radiated round that center. The focus of life turned inward.

In the creation myths of the Maya of Mexico, the gods made men and women from a simple lump of cornmeal. The Hopis of the Southwest say the creators made the first beings from ears of corn.

From the civilizations of Mexico they borrowed the most potent gods of rain to add to their pantheon. They celebrated Mesoamerican deities of fertility, but with a different face. Masked gods appeared among them in the plazas. The annual round of ceremonies devoted to corn and rain became the true sustenance of life.

When Southwestern tribes adopted rituals introduced by visitors from the south, they needed the proper accoutrements, copper bells and bright macaw feathers. "What is equal to the blues and greens of those brilliant feathers?" they asked.

No one remembers who found the first turquoise stone. Some say it fell to earth. Others say the stone was lying on the sand with its eye open. Coyote came along, picked it up, and threw it in the air. And so the sky was made. The sky is an immense blue stone that breaks in summer and pours forth rain. Black matrix is the net that holds the sky together and the deep blue is the bird within it. The stone is the egg, a room without a roof, the trace of the first sea, the map of the journey.

Scattered groups of Anasazi farmers happened to be living on a dry sea in the shadow of a mountain of turquoise, near present-day Santa Fé. The stone served as offerings to the gods and as adornments for the priests. It served as a charm and a symbol of life. In exchange for blue and green feathers, the Anasazis offered blue stones and green stones to the southern merchants, and it was considered a fair trade. By A.D. 1000 men were laboring in the turquoise mines and artisans at Chaco Canyon were polishing stones for nobles of lands they would never see. On the accumulated wealth of ritual goods Chaco Canyon became the preeminent culture of the Southwest. The fortunes of the Anasazis rested in the sacred dance, and the sway of civilizations that rose and fell in giant swells across the desert ocean.

On the Plains of San Agustin looms the Very Large Array, a series of radio telescopes, white as salt lakes, revolving on a motionless seabed. From the edge of the universe come voices as they emerge from caves, blending with voices of the archaeologists of deep space, shouts of hunters, traders as they barter, and women singing the ordinary news of the day.

The sweeping Sonoran Desert was the birthplace of the ancient Desert Culture. For five thousand years the seeds of mesquite, juniper, and piñon and the fruits of the saguaro and prickly pear sustained the nomadic hunter-gatherers of the Tonto Basin in southern Arizona. Sophisticated Hohokam farmers settled in the basin around A.D. 700, followed by the Salado people.

A half moon in the steep slopes rising above the Salt River shelters a deserted Salado village of rock and mud. The Salado prospered here for three hundred years before moving on.

The Salado people who occupied this village in the cliffs cultivated corn, beans, and amaranth in irrigated fields on the river plain below. Reaching beyond their isolated community, they traded cotton for shells from the Gulf of California and macaw feathers from Mexico. The Salado abandoned their home during the widespread upheavals of 1450. View from inside cliff dwelling, Tonto National Monument, Arizona.

Veins of blue and green turquoise run under the Cerrillos hills near Santa Fé. Stones from Turquoise Mountain went west to Chaco Canyon and south to the civilizations of Mexico. When the Spaniards arrived in the sixteenth century, the Indians risked body and soul to supply gemstones for Spain's nobility. The Tiffany Mine continues to yield fine turquoises.

Blue as water,
green as a dollar,
rock of fortune
and the rock of
love. They work
like a charm, these
turquoise gems
in the rough.

The macaw is brighter than the phoenix. His feathers travel farther than the macaw can fly. Throughout Mesoamerica his plumage is an essential part of ceremonial regalia. In Pre-Columbian times, the people of the Southwest traded turquoise for macaw feathers. The mythic bird is identified with the sun, fire, and turquoise.

Peyote-style fixed fan of scarlet macaw feathers. Lana Bati, Navajo, 1988. Jeff Lewis' Trade Roots Collection, Ramah, New Mexico.

Overleaf:

Spider Woman created the Hero Twins out of earth and spit. Ash Boy raised the mountains; Echo tuned the vibratory centers of the world. The twins live at the opposite poles of the earth, to keep the world spinning. Monument Valley, Utah.

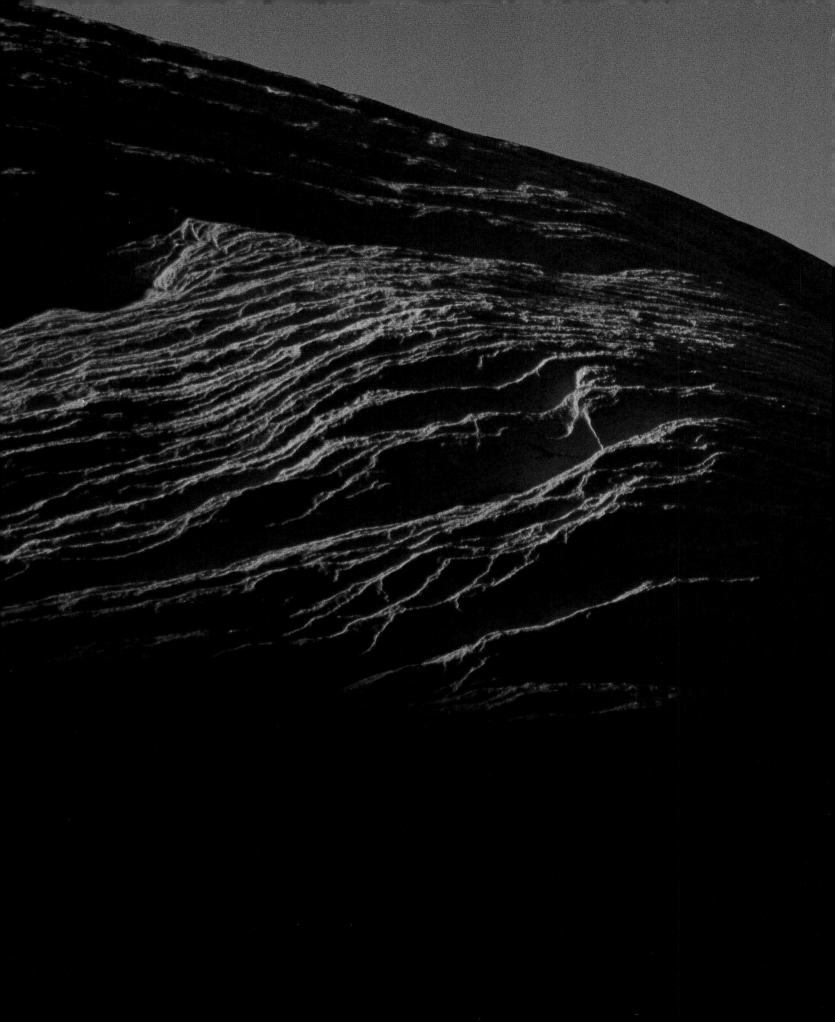

Tides of water and wind create living bones of sandstone. So many Western movie heroes have ridden palominos across this monumental backdrop, so many runaway stagecoaches have carried off damsels in distress, it is easy to forget that the monolithic buttes are part of the homeland of the Navajos. Monument Valley, Utah.

Ever since First Man, people have been giving rocks foolish names, to cut them down to size. The monolith called Mexican Hat named the Arizona town right by it. Folks don't mind living under a big sombrero. Mexican Hat is a hoodoo creased by wind. When the wind blows, the rock answers, "Hoo-Doo."

Overleaf:

A round ceremonial kiva represents the Place of Emergence, where the ancestors of the Pueblos emerged from the underworld to the surface of the earth. Pueblo ruins and walls of the San Gregorio de Abo Church, built by Franciscan missionaries in 1622, waste together in sun and wind, monuments to separate cultures and beliefs. Pueblos extracted salt from the vast lake beds of the Salinas Valley. The Spanish found gold in the nearby Sandia Mountains and drew salt from the lakes, which they sent by mule-train to Mexico. Defenseless against raiders from the Plains, the pueblo and the mission were abandoned around 1673.

The ruins of Nuestra Señora de la Purisima Concepcion de Cuarac reign over the Salinas Valley. Erected by Franciscan missionaries in 1627, the church was abandoned in 1677 by priests and Indians alike after severe drought and Apache raids.

After a thousand years as a cross-roads between Mesoamerica and the Southwest, Casas Grandes ends in a maze. At its height in 1300, Casas Grandes was a vital trading center in the northern desert of Chihuahua, Mexico. Inhabitants produced copper bells and bred macaws, which merchants traded for turquoise. Through Casas Grandes the gods and rituals of Mesoamerica traveled north to the Pueblos.

The Tyuonyi cliff dwellings in Frijoles Canyon retreat into the volcanic tufa ridge. Five hundred years erase the differences between a house, a cave, and a swallow's nest. Anasazi architects molded a pure aesthetic at one with rock and wind. Bandelier National Monument, New Mexico.

Wild datura blooms
at the foot of a
ladder leading to
a round kiva made
of song. Bandelier
National Monument.

Overleaf:

White House lies
in a great swirl
of the river of
Canyon de Chelly.
The Anasazis
migrated here
before the fall of
Chaco Canyon,
seeking shelter in
the red cliffs made
by Spider Woman.
The Anasazis left
their mark onthe
walls and then
flowed on to
settle along the
Rio Grande.

Above and opposite:

Long ago the forests turned to stone, and now the fallen trees are polished jasper, amethyst, quartz, and agate, the colors of autumn leaves and the color of the earth they deserted. Petrified Forest National Park, Arizona.

Overleaf:

Changing Woman
stirred the waters,
and mountains
grew from foam.
Higher they rose,
swirling in rivers
of clouds and
changing with
the wind, just like
the gods. Valley
of the Gods, near
the Mokee
Dugway, Utah.

From the Four Corners, where Utah, Colorado, Arizona, and New Mexico meet, the Anasazis came to worship in the Great Kiva of Pueblo Bonito. In every direction, ceremonial roads ran from the center to villages beyond Chaco Canyon. Turquoise bound them to the Toltecs, Tarascans, Mixtecs, and Maya of Mexico. After 150 years of unprecedented prosperity, the Anasazis abandoned the canyon in 1150, carrying their creative gifts to more fertile soil. Pueblo Bonito at Chaco Canyon, New Mexico.

A T-shaped door-way at Chaco Canyon leads to mystery. This Southwestern architectural feature, seen at Mesa Verde and Casas Grandes, resembles the form of doors and windows at Mesoamerican sites to the south, the form of the rectangular kiva, and the form of a man's face and body. Theories abound. The shape made it easier for bearers to maneuver heavy bundles through the door. The idea was introduced by Mexican architects and merchants. The door was the right form for the god of wind to enter without a sound. Chaco Canyon.

In the desert, minerals and the sparse world of vegetation are interchangeable. Walk along the dry arroyo and see piñon-green serpentine, white quartz translucent as wild datura, pink rhodochrosite faint as Apaches' tears.

In the foothills of the Sangre de Cristo Mountains, Pecos played a strategic role in the turquoise and shell trade among the Pueblos and tribes of northern Mexico and the High Plains. The Franciscan mission loomed above the ancient pueblo until Pecos fell to Comanche raiders in the eighteenth century. Pecos National Monument, New Mexico.

Echo made the earth an instrument of music in praise of the creator. Mountains quaked. The great volcanic dike raised long rumbling chords.

"Rock with Wings" resounds across Navajoland. Shiprock, New Mexico.

Dwarfed by a spectacular amphitheater, whose cathedral roof rises 200 feet above the empty village, Betatakin weathers the seasons of the canyonlands of northern Arizona. The Anasazis arose east of this arid region and spread throughout the Southwest. The farmers of Betatakin remained poor relations of their ambitious urban relatives at Chaco Canyon. They lived within the grand landscape that eventually humbled Anasazi culture. Navajo National Monument, Kayenta, Arizona.

Above the brown desert lies the blue desert of the sky. The two deserts meet in a long strand on Enchanted Mesa. They meet at the corners of the houses of the City in the Sky. The blue of doors and windows ward off evil. Blue attracts the beneficent ancestral spirits, who dwell above this island. Without blue frames the 800-year-old houses of Acoma would disappear.

The Navajos can
put a hundred
miles of breathing
space between
themselves and
their next-door
neighbors.
Isolated hogans
dot a vast land-
scape, marked at
each cardinal
point by a sacred
mountain and a
turquoise at the
center.

Big River in the
United States,
Strong River in
Mexico, the Rio
Grande is border-
land, homeland.
Like all great
rivers, the Rio
Grande nourishes
life and imagina-
tion for all who
live along its
route. Constant,
it waters the dust.
Powerful at its
source, it plunges
out of the Rockies
and divides the
desert. Rio Grande
Gorge, near Taos,
New Mexico.

CHAPTER 2

THE ROAD
FROM THE HEART
OF THE EARTH

The trails of the ancestors blazed a giant matrix over the desert. Those trails are invisible—footprints planted in sand erased by devils in the wind. All legends of journeys through wilderness are words for the wind, suspended in time, generation after generation.

Across the American Southwest and the land of Mexico are enduring signs of passage: choirs of water jars, whorls of the potter's hand on sherds of sunbaked clay, strands of beads, tribes of smiling figurines. Beyond the valley may lie a ruined city. Each perfect hill may hold a pyramid, turquoise stones, gold rings, feathers—a ragged history book made of figbark paper with small, inkblack footprints drawn across the pages.

"We came from the north," the pages read, from Aztlán, Lake of Snowy Egrets, Place of Seven Caves. Other accounts say they came from Tamoanchan, Land of Rain and Mists, crossing the Mountain of Masks in search of the seven caves of their original home. If nomads pursued the tracks of big game, they failed to record that in their epic journey. Their wandering course, stories say, followed the flights of eagles and the obsidian butterfly.

The desert dwellers discovered watered valleys, steaming coasts, and tropical foliage. Divided by natural boundaries, the common pattern of their lives slowly split into hundreds of distinctive cultures. Then they retraced their steps, crossing rivers and ranges to find rare commodities, exchange ritual objects, or seek inspiration. The most intrepid travelers forged trails of shells, trails of feathers, trails of salt, cotton, and maize, trails of jade, gold dust, and turquoise.

Bands of Chichimecs in the northern desert continued a bare hunter-gatherer existence. Tribes that moved farther south discovered the basic ingredient for stability—corn—and shared it with their neighbors. Eventually they settled down, became farmers, built villages, and began making pottery, about 1500 B.C. Great city-states and trading empires sprang up in succession. Certain commonalities united the cultures of Mesoamerica and their relatives in the Southwest: diet, a calendar, astronomy and mathematics, some form of hieroglyphic writing, religious beliefs, and games. Beginning with the Olmecs, jade ritual objects conveyed fundamental cultural ideas. After A.D. 1000, turquoise from the northern periphery assumed wide economic and symbolic significance.

Communication routes created the most permanent avenues of alliance. Trade networks weathered the collapse of Classic civilization in A.D. 900, forged a semblance of unity during the turbulent post-Classic era, and survived the Conquest. Drought, earthquakes, military defeat, some flaw in the power of men, or some innate restlessness forced

**Aztec ancestors emerging from
Place of Seven Caves**

people to move on. Tracing their migrations is like following a hummingbird in flight. The flow of populations, like the rise and fall of civilizations, is the theme of Mesoamerican myth and history and the theme of time.

Movement, the Aztecs believed, was the essence of the cosmos; the name of the fifth creation. A footprint on the road was the Maya metaphor for the beginning of time.

In the Maya epic of creation, *Popol Vuh*, the hero twins, Hunahpu and Xbalanque, play a ballgame with the nine lords of death. Through tricks, magic, and self-sacrifice, they banish death to the underworld and then rise as Venus and the sun. The ballgame was re-created endlessly, played by kings and celebrated in art as a triumphal rite of rebirth. Yet death had a way of crawling under the skin. This, too, the artists depicted: death splitting the body in two, death riding on people's backs, death making his fixed rounds in the calendar. Astronomers and mathematicians charted vast cycles of time to accommodate him. Sculptors carved gods of corn and rain in order to transcend him. Smiths cast golden gods of spring and fashioned turquoise mosaics to mask the gods of thunder, fire, war, and morning star. These works are the shining bones of Mesoamerican civilization.

Bones are seeds, wrote the Maya scribes. Life in rural Mexico has not changed substantially for thousands of years. The Indians go on practicing the same rituals, speaking the old languages, and planting mountains in corn. "People may perish," said Maryan Peres, a Maya shaman, praying for peace in the Middle East. "The earth will remain."

Years are stones, in the languages of the Aztecs and Maya, round as the sun and immutable. When John Lloyd Stephens, an American lawyer, and British artist Frederick Catherwood came upon the Maya ruins of Copán, Honduras, in 1841, they discovered pyramids toppled by enormous roots. One monument leaned in the stillness like "a divinity mourning over a fallen people." They asked the Indians who had built the mysterious city, and their answer was "Quién sabe?"—Who knows?

In the eternal present, history and myth reflect back and forth in a dark obsidian mirror. Mexican civilization, whose age reaches back at least three thousand years and shines forward through repeated glory and disaster, is a still point of light. In this separate reality, all events are motionless and occur at the same time. What seems a form of cultural amnesia is a small victory over death.

The people called the Olmecs lived between green waters, jetblack estuaries, and the netherworld. Olmec cities emerged fullblown, with no known antecedents. By 1200 B.C. the Olmecs were carving the most masterful jades in the world. When archaeologists working in central Mexico in the 1930s traced extraordinary jade figurines to Olmec sites five hundred miles away on the coast of Veracruz, they were convinced they had found the "mother culture" of Mexico, progenitor of the Maya, Nahua, Zapotec, Toltec, and Aztec civilizations. The last culture discovered was the first.

Olmec art has birth as its central theme. In stone monuments, men awaken from the jaws of serpents; priests lean at the mouths of caves, cradling in their arms a crying child, half human, half jaguar. Jade masks, pendants, and figurines bear this were-jaguar image: a scowling feline face with a deep saurian cleft across the head atop a chubby, sexless baby body grasping the air with angry claws.

Olmec culture is pivotal: the supreme expression of thousands of years of archaic belief and the solemn awakening of New World civilization.

The Olmecs evolved the Long Count calendar, which begins on the apparently mythical date of 3113 B.C. As they gave a measured form to time, they gave a shape to words through hieroglyphic writing and an arithmetical order to things through a simple way of recording numbers in bars and dots. Of equal significance, the Olmecs invented a game like soccer played with a rubber ball. From Central America to Arizona, the game became an irrepressible sport, occasion for gambling and ultimate risk, the central arena for deadly combat between rival kings and a mystical tournament between gods.

The Olmecs shared these discoveries through migrations and through trade. Boats plied the cypress swamps, ferrying strings of merchants carrying cargoes of jade, hematite, turquoise, obsidian, amethyst, and amber to the island city of La Venta down the Tonala River. From their heartland the Olmecs walked westward, over the slopes of the volcano Orizaba to the villages on Lake Texcoco. From their base in the state of Guerrero, they brought jades to the people of West Mexico and the Pacific coast. At Tlatilco, Olmec were-jaguars seem at home among clay figurines of acrobats, ballplayers, and a remarkable population of hunchbacks and freaks. On a cliff face rising above the trade center of Chalcatzingo, in the state of Morelos, the portrait of an Olmec king rules from his throne.

Seeking magnetite mirrors, the Olmecs trekked across the windswept Isthmus of Tehuantepec and settled in the long river valley of Oaxaca. The Zapotec center of Monte Albán commanded the valley. The evolution of a Zapotec calendar and hieroglyphics about the same time that the Olmecs began inscribing dates, names, and places on stone suggests cross-cultural exchange between them as early as 1000 B.C.

As the Olmecs moved south through the mountains of Chiapas, along the Pacific, and into Guatemala, major cultures sprang up in their wake: Chiapa de Corzo, Izapa, Kaminaljuyú, and Uaxactun. Olmec traders journeyed as far as Costa Rica, where they found the finest source of jade.

Canoes must have carried the Olmecs around the shores of the Gulf of Mexico to the Mississippi Delta. They sang in the bayous the song of the jaguar and rattler. They paddled up the muddy water into the heart of North America. On the outskirts of St. Louis, the exhausted, homesick sailors acquired axes and left behind their pots.

Wherever they traveled, the Olmecs left their mark on the arts of surrounding cultures. The Jade Route, as Michael Coe calls it, was a political road as well, binding chiefs of farflung states to allegiances with Olmec rulers. Jade ornaments of the were-jaguar confirmed the temporal and supernatural power of leaders, who, as royal shamans, transformed literally into jaguar-kings. Jade, "the heart of earth," and the jaguar, symbol of the underworld and source of rain, became emblems of rulership and the divine right of kings.

Olmec merchants were political, cultural, and religious emmissaries, pathfinders for future cultures. The obsidian mirrors they carried were magical emblems of fire and clairvoyance, believed to light the way of underworld travelers. Stars were the jaguar's spots, and the spots formed the road.

As mysteriously as they had appeared, the Olmecs vanished, around 300 B.C. They entered the realm of myth as slayers of giants, and their homeland became the paradisal Tamoanchan. Olmec jades were treasured by Maya and Aztec kings, worn by rulers of Teotihuacán on the highest ceremonial occasions, and presented as offerings to Tlaloc, god of rain. Over time, the mask of the werejaguar would evolve into a sacred serpent or toad, the eyes, fangs, and flashing brows become prominent features of other deities. Olmec eyes gaze inward. The downcast mouth growls. The jaguar god of rain is a god of tears.

The sea, gate to the Otherworld, bound the Maya world, and its red tides flowed within them. The Maya may have migrated from the coast of Oregon and northern California, settling in the highlands of Guatemala by 3000 B.C.—the beginning, coincidentally, of their calendar. There they divided into separate tribes and dispersed to the four directions, settling along the Gulf Coast of Tamaulipas and Veracruz, throughout the Yucatán, Chiapas, Guatemala, and as far south as El Salvador.

By their own accounts, the Maya traced their lineage to the Olmecs. Despite differences in language and chronic xenophobia, the Maya borrowed the icons of the jaguar, serpent, and toad. They adopted the Olmec number system of bars and dots, elaborated on the Long-Count calendar, and developed hieroglyphic symbols into the most complex writing system in the world. They patterned their culture and political system after the Olmec, claiming descent from a legendary ancestor, Lord Knot-Skull, who reigned during Olmec times.

The Maya began building public centers around 200 B.C. Supported by swidden agriculture and movable fields, independent city-states flourished throughout the lowlands. The Classic Maya never formed a unified empire. Instead, a kind of cooperative anarchy prevailed. Yet kings exerted enough cohesiveness to bind a mosaic of city-states into one of the most enduring civilizations in Mesoamerica.

Political power and the arts evolved together. The Maya reverence for art and writing is reflected in the *Popol Vuh*. The older brothers of the Hero Twins, Hunahpu and Xbalanque, were the twin brothers I Artisan and 1 Monkey. Chuen, the monkey god, was the deity of art and pleasure. The four Pauahtuns, or "Wind Stones," who upheld the world, were the patron deities of writers. With these sources of inspiration, the Maya artist enjoyed a certain freedom of expression, imbuing works with raw humor, inventiveness, and revelation. The gods gave shape to man, and artists gave form to the gods.

The purpose of public art was to display the divinity of kings. Posed in full regalia, the king was the measure of divine grace, his head often turned in profile, as if listening to the world on the other side. Priest, warrior, incarnation of the sun and Venus, he bore the titles Great Sun-faced Lord, Maize Lord, Lord of the Tree, Ballplayer. He was the center of the cosmos.

The magic of the king depended on the skills of Maya artists and scribes. The dramatic beauty of the rites, the king's emblems, and his gorgeous attire were the works of artisans. The richness of each ritual object depended on materials from afar.

The Maya organized a system of long-distance trade. Dealing principally in elite goods, merchants supported the status of the ruling class and priesthood. Maya roads, the longest of which ran sixty-two miles between Cobá and Yaxuna in the Yucatán, were reserved for ceremonial processions of priests, nobles, and musicians playing rattles, drums, turtle shells, and conch trumpets.

Following dusty routes blazed by the Olmecs, Maya merchants journeyed to the Motagua Valley in Guatemala, where they secured the finest apple-green jade. They acquired metal work from Costa Rica, whose traders had acquired gold from Panama, Colombia, and Peru. They searched the shores of the Gulf and Caribbean for shells and stingray spines, paddled up inland rivers for feathers, journeyed to the Pacific to obtain chocolate to suit royal palates. Northern routes led to sources of green obsidian, pearls, and turquoise stones.

Some merchants may have been artisans. The high level of craftsmanship across the vast Maya region, the basic uniformity in style, and the standardization of symbols and hieroglyphic writing suggests the existence of traveling craftsmen who learned special skills at art centers like Copán or were commissioned to produce stelae or bas-reliefs at various cities within the Maya realm. The most noted artisans ventured off to paint at Teotihuacán.

Among the ranks of artists, bone carvers, potters, and scribes were itinerant dentists whose medium was enamel. For in addition to tattoos, body paint, crossed eyes, and elongated heads, Mesoamericans thought themselves most pleasing with front teeth filed to a T. If they could afford it, modish people hired jewelers to set round pyrite, jade, or turquoise stones in their teeth. This beaming fashion spread all the way to the Southwest.

Artisans held an honored position in Maya society. Members of the ruling class practiced the arts of painting and writing. Princes signed their works. The royal courts rang with music, dances, and brilliant dialogues among poets, priests, painters, and watchers of the stars. A noble brotherhood of artisans sustained the brotherhood of kings.

In the Valley of Mexico, east of the great lake that once mirrored snow-capped volcanic peaks and drew deer and water birds to its shores, lay Teotihuacán, City of the Gods. The legendary city was the birthplace of the Fifth Sun, and there kings

Ek Chuah, Maya god of merchants

ascended to the realm of the gods. A revered place of pilgrimage, all roads led to Teotihuacán.

At its heart rose the Temple of the Sun, a massive mountain of stone resting above seven underground caves, the sacred place of emergence. From this symbolic center the ceremonial Avenue of the Dead, lined with royal tombs, led toward the royal precinct, administrative center, and Temple of Quetzalcoatl, the Feathered Serpent.

The people who commanded this great metropolis were Nahua speakers from the northern desert. Once nomadic, they managed to rally villagers living on the Central Plateau of Mexico and organized vast irrigation systems that guaranteed plentiful harvests and wealth. Teotihuacán, at its height in A.D. 450, was populated by 150,000 people who resided in multistory houses within the main city and its suburbs. Broad thoroughfares stretched toward the surrounding mountains. Palaces shone in vivid hues of maroon, green, and turquoise blue. The downtown contained markets, businesses, and separate wards for potters, stonecutters, and obsidian workers. Streets swarmed with visitors from every part of Mexico. Zapotec, Puebla, and Maya artisans took up life in the big city. Teotihuacán was the navel of Mexico, the center of an expansive religious, commercial, and military empire.

Among the deities who blessed the austere opulence of the state was Yacatecutli, patron of

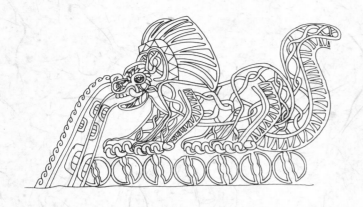

**Jaguar with feathered headdress,
Teotihuacán**

merchants. Teotihuacán controlled a wide trading network that reached into the Southwest and Guatemala. A special class of long-distance merchants traveled in search of rare goods and ritual objects. Potters produced export wares that were stackable and easily transportable in tumplines. They mass-produced religious figurines for distribution. Portable stuccoed vases, bearing images of the gods, carried the religious and artistic message of Teotihuacán to cultures north and south. The heaviest traffic was in obsidian, honed into weapons, tools, transparent earspools, and delicate instruments for blood letting sacrifices. The ancient obsidian trade linked Teotihuacán and Oaxaca.

As Teotihuacán rose to power, Monte Albán became a major center with strongholds throughout the Valley of Oaxaca. Yet its inhabitants never penetrated far beyond the region. The Zapotecs were by nature isolationists, and the city's architects had chosen a promontory with a strategic view. They invited cultural and commercial exchanges with Teotihuacános to the north and Maya to the south.

The turquoise symbol appears for the first time in Zapotec hieroglyphs. The stone and the blue pigment it yielded held special significance to the artisans and nobles of the region. Turquoise may have come from yet undiscovered sources near the Isthmus of Tehuantepec, a vital crossroads controlled

by the Zapotecs. Or perhaps it was brought from the distant Southwest via Teotihuacano trade.

The merchants of Teotihuacán pushed eight hundred miles south of Oaxaca, dominated the Maya of the Guatemalan highlands, and colonized Kaminaljuyú, where Guatemala City now stands. Architects turned that city into a small replica of Teotihuacán. The local governors who controlled the cacao trade enjoyed a lavish lifestyle, surrounded in this world and in the afterlife with painted vessels, jades, pyrite mirrors, pearls, and ornate textiles from central Mexico and the coast of Veracruz.

Moving into the Maya heartland, Teotihuacán established commercial ties with Tikal, the most powerful of the lowland Maya city-states and at the center of the Maya sphere. Teotihuacános coveted quetzal feathers and Maya polychrome export wares, while the Maya imported rare green obsidian blades, essential for bloodletting rituals.

Trade heightened political and military alliances. Capitalizing on hostilities among the lowland Maya cities, Teotihuacán stationed mercenaries there who helped Tikal vanquish her rivals and introduced a style of combat that undermined the Maya pattern of warfare. Wide-scale military escalation ultimately led to the fall of Classic civilization.

Teotihuacán extended its trading sphere to West Mexico, a region with access to the Pacific coastal route and sources of obsidian, and advanced the borders of Mesoamerica as far as Zacatecas. The frontier towns of La Quemada and Alta Vista had a long history prior to intensive contact with Teotihuacán. These modest settlements were more than a buffer against the barbaric Chichimecs. The region was rich in raw minerals.

There dwelled the pioneers, outlaws, and artists, the strict, the congenitally dull, those who clutched their purse strings, those who had never tasted chocolate or had any need for fancy clothes, the forlorn, the hermits, the exiles, priests who had neglected their vows, people who ate dog meat, people who stacked skulls, braggarts, miners, gamblers, small-time peddlars, those who rubbed elbows with foreigners and ate their awful food.

The roads leading to La Quemada welcomed all visitors—"city slickers" from the south, barbarians from the north. A civilized outpost in the bend of La Quemada River, the city was a harbor where strangers could feel at ease, talk openly, and trade.

The province owed its true character to the mineral wealth surrounding it. Alta Vista, center of the Chalchihuites culture, had supported mining operations for centuries. Chalchihuites ("Blue Stones") was the first Mesoamerican culture to exploit and work turquoise. Lapidaries created turquoise mosaic discs, rings, beads, and pendants, primarily for prestige burials. Turquoise ornaments may have been sent to Teotihuacán. As demand for turquoise increased, prospectors from Alta Vista began searching for new sources. Exploratory expeditions took them into the Southwest. By A.D. 700, Alta Vista was importing turquoise from the Cerrillos mines, outside Santa Fé. Exploitation of this rare Southwestern resource was a major stimulus for social and economic growth among the Hohokam and Anasazi cultures.

Artisans of the region were producing other vital objects for ritual use and trade: pseudo-cloisonné vases, decorated with images of the god Tezcatlipoca, Lord of the Smoking Mirror. The mosaic-like ceramic form was perfected by artisans of Teuchtitlan, near Lake Chapala in West Mexico. While artisans at Teotihuacán painted the stuccoed surface of pots, the craftspeople of La Quemada and Alta Vista inlaid cells with separate colors. They had abundant supplies of red, blue, green, and yellow pigments, ground from hematite, azurite, malachite, limonite, and cinnabar mined in the mountains nearby. Surplus pigments ground from turquoise were prized by the fresco painters working at Teotihuacán.

The mines were hot; dust and swirling smoke from burning torches choked the air, bats swarmed in the grave tunnels. This was the land of Tezcatlipoca: his smoking mirror lit the foul passages of the underworld.

Feathered dancer, pseudo-cloisonné, Teuchtitlán

The people of the provinces of Teotihuacán were rugged keepers of tradition. The gentle folk who live in those parts today, with their deep appreciation for art, may have come by their sensibility through terminal loneliness, accumulated lifetimes of hammering rock in utter blackness until the rocks yielded the intense green and rare blue that colored the visions of paradise glowing on the walls of the royal chambers of Teotihuacán.

Working under the open sky, the craftsmen of La Quemada and Alta Vista were connoisseurs of shades of blue, tones of green. Accustomed to mirages, they could see the footprints of the one-legged god of magic and war, Tezcatlipoca. Artists and outcasts, they were biding their time.

Across the northern plateau at the edge of Mesoamerica stretched an empty expanse of mountains, grasslands, and desert. Northern Mexico, according to Aztec chroniclers, was the domain of wild men. They wore animal skins, lived in caves, and eked out a pitiful existence collecting mesquite seeds and hunting rabbits with bow and arrow. They felt no compulsion to develop pottery or the loom, tend fields, build cities, or shape stone or clay into images of themselves or the gods. Little is known about these nomads beyond what the Aztecs tell us. The many bands roaming the north were called Chichimecs, "People of the Dog."

Maize first traveled from central Mexico to the Southwest with the hunters and foragers of the region. The crop stabilized the route. Some bands of Chichimecs lived as occasional farmers along the slopes of the Sierra Madre Occidental. These groups adopted pottery and village life and formed a chain of communities between Mesoamerica and the Southwest that lasted until 1450. Their descendants, the Tepehuana, Papago, Opata, and Tarahumara, occupy roughly the same region today.

Shells, turquoise, pottery, and clay figurines passed, like rumors, from village to village. Mesoamerican inventions like the ballgame probably reached the Southwest through competitions. The spread of ceremonial architecture required a more formal system of contact and social organization.

Increasing trade enriched the cultures of Chalchihuites and the Hohokam of southern Arizona. Having established a relatively prosperous way of life based on irrigation, the Hohokam developed a sophisticated craft tradition, producing an enormous variety of shell ornaments, stone bowls, and stone axes. Master craftsmen, the Hohokam lent and borrowed selectively. That religious concepts linked the people of the Southwest and Mesoamerica is suggested by finds like iron pyrite mirrors, pseudo-cloisonné pieces, and turquoise mosaics at Snaketown, near Phoenix, by A.D. 700. Images of Tezcatlipoca appear on ceremonial

objects; images of the Horned Serpent on rock faces. Blessed with material comfort and ingenuity and receptive to the outside world, the Hohokam were prepared to expand.

The Chichimecs to the south also were in an expansionary phase. Possessing the vigor that dissipates with sedentary life, the barbarians lurked at the Mesoamerican border, agents of destruction and harbingers of a more militant culture.

Teotihuacán fell to the northern invaders in A.D. 700. A long period of drought may have rendered the state's control over irrigation useless, weakening the authority of the ruling class and undermining the faith of the population. Nomadic tribes seized the opportunity. They burned the city, left the palaces in ruins, and took up residence in the hollow rooms. The city's inhabitants fled, some migrating as far north as Alta Vista.

So many disparate tribes wandered through central Mexico, it is nearly impossible to trace their movements. Nahuas, Toltecs, Chichimecs, Mixtecs, Pueblas, and Maya exchanged blows, exchanged cities. They had everything, and nothing, in common: a confusion of gods, overlapping myths. Tensions created a transformation that wedded religious symbols from West Mexico to the Maya region. From the hands of Mixtec-Puebla craftsmen, who descended from artisans of Teotihuacán, emerged a pan-American art style.

Along the Gulf of Mexico, cities that once had influenced the decorative arts of Teotihuacán and reaped the benefits of reciprocal trade grew in importance. The "Classic Veracruz" cultures, despite proximity to ancient Olmec sites, possessed a refined art style that shows greater affinity with the baroque motifs of the Maya and Izapa civilizations. Figurines are robed in fine Maya-style designs. Stone axes and U-shaped yokes, ponderous ballgame gear, are found at distant Maya sites in El Salvador. Maya myths reaching the Southwest filtered through these cities, a relatively short journey from Texas.

The Veracruz cultures had a fixation on the ballgame. The enormous site of El Tajin, in the lush vanilla-growing country of northern Veracruz, had at least seven ball courts, built above the abode of the lords of thunderstorms. Scenes of the ballgame, including graphic depictions of the final sacrificial beheading, suggest that El Tajin rose to greatness at the expense of numerous captured rulers. Walls of temples, palaces, and ball courts bristle with the god of death, skulls, and bones.

Their immediate neighbors at Remojadas to the south depicted smiling boys and girls holding hands. They are a tiny nation of joyful friends in the midst of warring cultures.

By A.D. 900 disintegration was everywhere. Warfare, political collapse, ecological ruin, abandonment of city after city: Monte Albán, Palenque, Tikal, Copán. Inhabitants held the end-of-cycle ceremony, broke up their households, and moved on.

Stone monuments tell the story, long narratives cut into them, row after row: the oratory of sun, moon, and stars; the rhetoric of jaguars and parrots, the double-headed serpent, earth monster, and long-lipped rain god; the puns and double-entendres; the games of words, the play of myth and history, a language that is both image and sound, recounting the saga of the universe:

And it came to pass
as night follows day...

Barbarians poured out of the desert of northern Mexico, bands of cavemen, tribes of Chichimecs, hunters stinking in animal skins, waving bows and arrows. With them ran refugees from outposts like La Quemada and Alta Vista. Toltec warriors joined them. The Toltec leader Mixcóatl, "Cloud Serpent" or "Milky Way," gathered these ragged tribes together and his warriors swept down like jaguars, serpents, and eagles into central Mexico.

A son was born to Mixcóatl in the year 1 Reed (A.D. 937). Unlike his father, Topiltzin was a contemplative, devoted to prayer and penance. The high priest of the cult of the Feathered Serpent, he took the name of Quetzalcoatl. As king he led his people to the city of Tula, where he built temples of turquoise, pearls, and coral. Patron of the arts, he

Eagle, Mixtec codex

introduced writing and metalwork. A pacifist, he forbade human sacrifice; he advised his worshippers to offer snakes and butterflies. He shut himself up in the palace, a god who refused to show his face.

Tula was a wondrous land, glorified by Aztec poets. Ears of corn grew big as milling stones and fields were rainbows of every color of cotton. The palaces were adorned with jade, turquoise, gold, and quetzal feathers. The works of metalsmiths were of surpassing beauty.

The legend of Quetzalcoatl, as culture hero and patron of the arts, has the ring of truth. Craftspeople from Northwest Mexico may have participated in the Toltec invasion and brought their skills in the lapidary art. Turquoise became the stone of the gods.

The Toltecs also brought their god Tezcatlipoca, patron of warriors and the enemy of Quetzalcoatl. History became a play between the forces of light and darkness, of religious unity and earthly strife.

In the year A.D. 987, a man named Topiltzin Quetzalcoatl came from the west and invaded Chichén Itzá, the most powerful Maya city in the Yucatán. Defeated by followers of Tezcatlipoca, he had fled Tula, marched or sailed along the Gulf Coast, and then stormed the city. Under the Toltec regime, the Maya erected a colonnaded temple dedicated to the

Birth of Quetzalcoatl, Mixtec codex

eagle and jaguar warriors. *Chacmools,* reclining figures cut in stone, lay ready to receive human hearts. Skull racks and jaguars feeding on human hearts became dominant motifs.

Along with this pernicious militancy, the Toltecs introduced an international outlook. The Maya, compelled to assume a more outgoing attitude toward foreigners, grew into a more expansive commercial empire. A new merchant elite, the Chontal Maya, rose to economic and political ascendancy and controlled the Gulf coast area from Tabasco to the Yucatán. More than thirty shrines, serving as lookout beacons, dot the island of Cozumel and the coastline. Found on the island are the remains of stone storage areas and massive platforms where goods were prepared for shipment.

Huge trading canoes plied the waters along the coastal channels of Belize and traveled as far south as Costa Rica and Panama. The traders carried salt, honey, tobacco, and cacao, which was used as currency. The canoes bore embroidered textiles, and feathers for the nobility.

Post-Classic Maya art lost its intricate subtlety and refinement, but this decline made Maya thought and beliefs more accessible and broadly influential. The synthesis of Toltec and Maya iconography became a part of the pan-American art style, a force for spiritual unity in the midst of almost constant warfare.

As the Maya extended their commercial ventures south, the Toltecs of Tula expanded in the north. Eventually their power spread across central Mexico from the Atlantic to the Pacific coasts, and into the Southwest. "Nothing was too difficult for them," the Aztecs said of them. "No place with which they dealt was too distant."

Toltecs flowed along the Gulf Coast route into Texas, and on to the southeastern United States. Mesoamerican traits reached the Southwest through the central corridor and along the Pacific route.

After the fall of Teotihuacán and before the rise of the Toltecs, the cities of the north and west solidified their regional networks. Alta Vista maintained its dominance as an economic and ceremonial center. Its prominence may have been due originally to a small group of astronomers and priests from Teotihuacán. Turquoise workshops, mosaic work, pseudo-cloisonné, and the cult of Tezcatlipoca all thrived before the Toltecs came to power in central Mexico. The relatively humble City of Turquoise may have been a seedbed for post-Classic artistry.

The complexity of ceremonial objects reflects the intensity of contact among cultures. The Hohokam of the Southwest adopted Mesoamerican symbols such as earth monsters, bird-serpents, hero twin deities, and the double-headed serpent of the sun and Venus. When the Mogollon spread out from their high mountain valleys onto more arable lands in southern New Mexico, they began borrowing animal and human motifs from the Hohokam. The Mimbres branch of the Mogollon charged those motifs with graphic power. The mythical scenes depicted on Mimbres black-and-white bowls, particularly the adventures of twin heroes, are reminiscent of episodes in the Maya *Popol Vuh.* The Mimbres also had access to turquoise, which they carved into animal and bird fetishes.

The most dramatic changes in the Southwest occurred among the Anasazis. The Anasazis moved into Chaco Canyon, and their simple settlements began to blossom around A.D. 700. By 1050, the canyon sheltered large towns with multistoried stone dwellings, broad ceremonial plazas, and great kivas accommodating hundreds of worshippers. This sudden building program reflects a vigorous growth in architectural technology, a sophisticated level of social and political organization, and material prosperity. Most extraordinary is the system of roads that united outlying villages to the main centers in the canyon. The roads run as far as the New Mexican site of Aztec and beyond, to Mesa Verde in Colorado. From isolated hamlets, thousands of people joined together to build a regional center unprecedented in the Southwest. Like the city-states of Mesoamerica, the cohesive force was both spiritual and economic. Turquoise was at the heart of this dynamic transformation.

The Anasazis had been working turquoise since the time of Christ. At Chaco Canyon, hundreds of thousands of pieces lay on the ground when archaeologists discovered the abandoned town. Most of that turquoise came from Cerrillos. The quantities of turquoise found in burials are mere suggestions of the amount of turquoise used at Chaco Canyon. Of neighboring cultures, only Alta Vista matches that quantity. The comparison between Alta Vista and Chaco Canyon is apt in other respects. Artisans at Chaco Canyon made turquoise mosaics employing bevelled-edge technology developed earlier at Alta Vista, and like the craftsmen of Alta Vista, created a monopoly. The mosaics featured figures of Tezcatlipoca or of the Feathered Serpent.

Once the workshops at Chaco started producing mosaics, Chacoans began procuring turquoise from a number of sources hundreds of miles away and kept it for themselves; they stopped shipping raw turquoise south and instead produced polished ornaments for distribution.

Turquoise ornaments have been found at the Hohokam site of Snaketown in Arizona, at Guasave-Aztatlán on the Pacific coast, and at Ixtlan del Rio in West Mexico. These are the same areas that used pseudo-cloisonné vases. Enhancing that tradition, the Anasazis used pseudo-cloisonné to decorate the sandstone backs or frames of pyrite

Hero Twins and catfish, Mimbres

mosaic mirrors, thus doubling the potency of those ancient ceremonial objects. Decorated mirror backs were found at Snaketown, in such quantity that it is probable that the craft originated there. Mirror backs from a site near Casa Grande are adorned with birds of brilliant plumage and a figure of Tezcatlipoca wearing elaborate feathers and a mirror at his temple. A decorated knife may have been used for human sacrifice.

The presence of decorated pyrite mirrors, pseudo-cloisonné, and turquoise mosaics in the Southwest and depictions of the same deities on those works in northwestern and West Mexico, suggests a shared cultural tradition as firm as the hand and as deep as the imagination of the heart. The Southwest yielded gems most worthy for religious art, the adornment of the gods, and the journey of the soul.

The popularity of turquoise ritual objects extended as far south as the Yucatán. The first leg of the journey led south through Mogollon settlements to the little town of Casas Grandes. Turquoise flowed from Casas Grandes to Alta Vista and from there to the Toltec city of Tula. Turquoises eventually reached Mixtec-Puebla craftsmen of central Mexico. The stones were cut into tiny pieces, the size of ants, spread on a large white cloth, sorted, and matched. Over the months they were fitted

**Offering of twenty copper bells,
Mixtec codex**

together—four thousand rectangular serpent scales and four serpent's heads in profile. Laid on a ground of pink sandstone, the serpents were surrounded by flower petals of cinnabar. In the center, flecks of hematite formed a round gray mirror. This masterful mosaic was conveyed to Chichén Itzá, where it was laid in a stone box and buried under the stone altar inside the Temple of the Warriors, a jeweled offering to the Feathered Serpent.

After 1000, trade in turquoise was most prolific along the Pacific coastal route. A momentous discovery had been made: the people of West Mexico learned metallurgy. Metallurgy gave the West Mexicans a brilliant trade advantage. Small copper axes, like those found in South America, were mass-produced and used, not as tools of warfare, but as money. Smiths also mass-produced cast copper bells, which, strung together as bracelets or in multitiered necklaces, became a significant item of trade. From West Mexico copper bells moved up the coast to Guasave-Aztatlán, over the Sierra Madre to Casas Grandes, and to the Southwest.

Copper bells were the major trade item sent to the Hohokam and Anasazis in exchange for turquoise. Tarascan artisans polished turquoise beads and excelled at turquoise mosaics. Sky-blue stones set in gold show a refined sense of artistry that was prized throughout Mesoamerica. The artistic skills and economic acumen of the Tarascans brought West Mexico into the Mesoamerican mainstream. Through the Tarascans, the turquoise mosaic mirrors of the Hohokam and Anasazis influenced other artisans of Mesoamerica.

Farther south, in Oaxaca, a new center arose at Mitla, "Place of Rest." This city reveals temples and palaces built like large jewels: geometric motifs, laid in delicate stonework mosaics set into a red background. The Mixtecs, or "Cloud People," who usurped the city left a number of screenfold books which record their history, beginning in A.D. 692. Their ancestors, it is written, vanquished the Puebla area and subdued the Zapotecs of Oaxaca through marriage into the royal line. In 1045, the Mixtec leader, Lord 8 Deer, journeyed to Tula, where the Toltec king invested him with the emblem of rulership, a turquoise nose button. By 1350, the Mixtecs moved into the Valley of Oaxaca.

The invading Mixtecs had been developing their skills for centuries, and the city of Mitla represents their craftsmanship on a grand architectural scale. They became renowned as the finest goldsmiths and crafters in turquoise mosaic in Mexico. In some fantastic melding, the ancient god of fire Xiuhtecutli, the "Turquoise Lord," united with Xipe Totec, patron deity of goldsmiths. The greatest works issued from this amalgamation of divine elements.

At Monte Albán, "amidst a heap of bones," archaeologist Alfonso Caso discovered, "golden bells, pearls, jade beads, and innumerable little turquoise plaques." Among the treasures were a rock crystal goblet, obsidian ear spools as thin as paper, and exquisite jaguar bone carvings, one depicting in minute detail a world of mythic heroes embraced by a serpent with turquoise eyes. Mixtec geometric motifs and turquoise inlay resemble abstract designs produced in the Southwest, a source of the finest turquoise used by Mixtec craftsmen. With constant rivalries among warring kingdoms during the post-Classic period, artisans, it seemed, were holding together the world.

Among the seafaring merchants of the Yucatán the most enduring products were the most sacred: obsidian, jade, metalwork, and turquoise mosaics.

Although metal ornaments have been found in earlier Classic Maya sites in the lowlands, the Maya began importing quantities of objects made of copper and gold alloy—"tumbaga"—during the tenth century. Maya artisans did not possess the same dedication to metalwork as the Mixtecs or Tarascans. Yet detailed repoussé pieces, with scenes of rulers depicted in the Toltec-Maya style, have been found at the Well of Sacrifice at Chichén Itzá.

The turquoise mosaic sun disk mirror, bearing the image of the Feathered Serpent, became the emblem of royal power. In a historic irony, Quetzalcoatl became the cult symbol of petty kings and commercial tyrants like the Itzá. Gifts were tossed as offerings to the gods of rain lurking under the green waters of the Sacred Well. There the treasures lay—beads, obsidian, plaques, beaten kings, turquoise serpents of the sky—long after the destruction of Chichén Itzá, interminable revolts, and the Itzá slunk back to the forests.

Tula was sacked and burned to the ground by raiding tribes of Chichimecs in 1156–58. At the same time, Apaches and Navajos swept across the Colorado Plateau and attacked Mesa Verde, Canyon de Chelly, and Chaco Canyon. Athabascan hunters, they wore skins and carried animal fetishes.

In his workshop at Pueblo Bonito in Chaco Canyon, the master lapidary meditated on stone. For days he stared at its cracks and veins. Then he began to polish. For days he polished, and as he polished, the sky, clouds, and branches of the trees fell from the stone, cliffs crumbled, the trees lost their leaves. Blue dust piled up like the sky and white dust piled up like snow. Wind came out of the earth, the turquoise dust scattered, the trees shook, and clouds avalanched. As he polished, birds stopped singing and the rains began, and for days rain poured down like sharp needles that could penetrate a stone. Then the rains ceased, and it never rained again.

A merchant going south took the stones, and carried them off like a sack of sand. Then the town packed up and the people moved away.

Inserting the *Tecuhtli* (turquoise nose button), symbol of kingship, Mixtec codex

The cultural diaspora took the Anasazis west into the Hohokam area, south into the Mogollon region of the lower Rio Grande Valley and West Texas, and down into Chihuahua. The Mimbres culture dissolved at the same time. Some of the people of Chaco Canyon settled at Hopi, in the seven Zuñi towns, on the mesa of Acoma, and along the Rio Grande.

Another wave of nomads poured out of the northern Mexican desert. By 1230, they were vying for power in the Valley of Mexico. Last came the Aztecs, "the people whose face nobody knows." Their diety was Huitzilopochtli, god of the sun and of war. Savage warriors, they stole other people's wives. Expelled by the Chichimecs of Colhuacan after they had sacrificed the daughter of the chief, they moved on to the marshes of the Lake of the Moon. Huitzilopochtli had promised them a kingdom of riches, lands and cities from sea to sea which they would wrest, not through magic, but through war. Beside the lake the outcasts wept. And the god spoke to them. "This is the place of our rest and our greatness. I order that the city which will be queen of all others be called Tenochtitlán. This is Mexico!"

The Aztecs drained the swamps, founded the city of Tenochtitlán in 1345, and linked it to the island of Tlatelolco, which they established as a market

**Aztec migration,
early colonial Mexican codex**

center. Causeways moved like long spokes over the waters of the lake. The grand entrance to the city was lined with vendors selling cloth, jewels, and sweets, just as they do today. Under the rule of Itzcoatl, the Aztecs burned the books of the people they conquered, rewrote history, and proclaimed themselves as chosen people, heirs to the Toltecs. Within fifty years, the eagle and jaguar warriors conquered the Huastec region, swept into Oaxaca, and subdued the coastal area as far south as the Guatemalan border. Aztlán, their mythical home, may lie in the modern states of Nayarit or Michoacán. They may have come from the Southwest following the diaspora from Chaco Canyon. Once they established their capital, the Aztecs identified completely with Toltec culture.

In the alleys of the lapidaries, boys watched their fathers shape turquoise beads with a drill, sand, and water, as their fathers, true Toltec descendants, had done for generations. The turquoise stone contained fire, the secret curative of healing herbs, the smoke of comets, and the blue of the universe. Out of the stone the lapidaries made long pendants for the Turquoise Lord, god of fire, a new sceptre for the god of the sun, a new mask for Quetzalcoatl, and blue inlays for the skulls.

In the workshops of the palace, the name of the sun rang out from dawn to dusk. Poets sang of war and the glories of the eagle warriors. Silversmiths

quarreled, because silver was the moon. Meanwhile, the goldsmiths, whose metal was more pliable, continued hammering, "ton-ton-ton," day after day, for two *tons*, or years. By that time the war was over, 100,000 captives had been sacrificed, and the queen had gone to the fourth paradise. Perhaps the goldsmiths had foreseen this turn of events in the gleaming rays of sun striking metal. Instead of flowers and birds they had beat out in low relief a coiled feathered serpent, so imbued with serpentine power the victorious king took the gleaming pendant from the treasure rooms of the palace and wore it next to his heart.

The Aztec language of Nahuatl was the trading *lingua franca* during the fifteenth century. It was spoken at ports on the southern Gulf Coast where Aztec merchants met the seafaring trading canoes of the Chontal Maya. Spanish chroniclers report that the language the traders spoke at Acoma Pueblo in the Southwest was Nahautl.

Aztec long-distance merchants, the *pochtecas*, dominated international trade. In the villages women would wait, sometimes twenty days, for the merchants and rare goods they would be bringing. These long-distance merchants were a class apart; they held the same status as warriors, had their own judicial courts, lived in separate precincts of the city, and worshipped their own gods. They managed the market places, regulated prices, and tried thieves. Their high position in Aztec society was, like a guild, hereditary and their professional lives a secret. Women were admitted to their ranks. Although the merchants accumulated riches and power, they walked the streets in rags. Their hair fell to their loins. In exchange for cotton textiles and polished ornaments manufactured in Tenochtitlán, distant nobles presented merchants with jade stones the size of tomatoes, tortoise shells, amber lip plugs, guacamaya feathers, cochineal dyes, and jaguar pelts. Before the *pochtecas* set out with caravans of bearers and slaves, they received these parting words, "Remember nothing within thy house. Continue to travel."

The wandering merchants journeyed for months, sometimes years, over great distances, over desert, plains, and crags, warding off grave dangers and pledged not to make a profit. Often it was bitter commerce. Bandits attacked the caravans. Enemy tribes held them captive. Before they ventured into the hostile territory of Zinacantán, in the Chiapas highlands, the merchants learned the local Maya language and disguised themselves in the local costume so as to trade without losing their lives. Thenceforth, the itinerant merchants were called "disguised merchants." The traders made the strenuous journey to Zinacantán for reasons other than amber and quetzal feathers. "They sought land for the god Huitzilopochtli," Fray Bernadino de Sahagún tells us. "Secretly they saw and entered everywhere in Anahuac, to travel inspecting as disguised merchants."

The merchants who dealt in precious stones worshipped Quetzalcoatl, lord of winds, who wore turquoise mosaic earrings and a turquoise mask. Tlaloc, the rain god, carried a turquoise scepter. The serpent-shaped *atlatl* of Huitzilopochtli was made of blue turquoise. The solar year was a turquoise stone, *xiútl*. Fire was turquoise and the universe was turquoise. Turquoise adorned heaven and it adorned death. Turquoise represented the purity of spiritual growth.

Common turquoises, *xiútl*—"herb which lies sprouting"—have dull, dark faces; they were broken into pieces and used for adornments. Fine turquoise, *teuxiutl,* belongs to the gods and is pale and smoking, writes Sahagún. "The pure life is considered as a well-smoked precious turquoise."

Aztec tribute lists report that turquoises came from the the Pacific coast, northwestern Oaxaca, central Veracruz, and mines near Tula. The finest stones still originated in the Southwest.

The cultural florescence of the Pueblos after 1300 may have been due partly to the enormous demand for turquoise among the Aztecs. The Indians of the Southwest began mining in earnest, opening sources in the Mojave desert and southern Nevada.

Although Aztec and Salmon flourished for a time as trading centers, they never achieved the dominance of Chaco Canyon.

After the collapse of Chaco Canyon and the Mimbres culture in 1150, Casas Grandes emerged as an important center, a major hub for the procurement and distribution of turquoise destined for Mesoamerican markets. A system of trails, guarded by watch towers, led to and from Casas Grandes, which grew from a town to a city. Multistoried apartment structures rose up around the central plaza. Pyramids, round ceremonial platforms, collonnaded halls, and I-shaped ballcourts were patterned after the architecture at La Quemada. The city had its own water system. Artisans produced shell, turquoise, and copper jewelry, copper needles, and copper bells. Trade pottery from the Hohokam area influenced the local polychrome. Plumed serpents and macaws become popular design motifs on pottery. These designs and the feather trade supported ceremonies dedicated to the Feathered Serpent.

Through Casas Grandes, the gods of Mesomerica reached the Mogollon and the Pueblo of the Rio Grande. Representations of masked deities and mythological figures appear on polychrome pottery, in kiva murals, and in rock art. Tlaloc, Tezcatlipoca, Xiutecutli, and Quetzalcoatl, the four brothers of creation, fused with Pueblo gods of rain, wind, fire, sun, and war. Kachinas, messengers of the gods, became part of a rich and complex ceremonial life. But there was a major difference: everyone, not just the wealthy, began wearing turquoise. The Zuñis, some of whom may have come from Chaco Canyon, became major traders.

The Aztec trading system relied on long-distance merchants for securing ritual goods and depended on local leadership, whose powers were short-lived. The breakdown of a dominant center in the Southwest meant a greater spread of wealth among independent Pueblo groups—and greater flux.

The Pacific coastal route increasingly fell under the control of the Tarascans of West Mexico. Fearless warriors, armed with copper weapons, they succeeded in warding off repeated attacks by the Aztec jaguar and eagle knights. The Tarascans had a gift for organization. They conducted commerce in the manner of a modern international business, recognizing that economic goals would rally the state more than overt attempts at political subjugation. Through secret agreements with coastal provinces levied by the Aztecs, the Tarascans acted as middlemen supplying subject states with turquoise so they could pay their taxes. Through the tribute system, the Tarascans indirectly supplied the Aztecs with turquoise while militarily blocking their access to the Southwest. The secret alliance with subject cities on the coast of Oaxaca opened up a turquoise route to the Yucatán that completely bypassed Tenochtitlán.

If Aztec *pochtecas* traveled the inland route along the eastern corridor of the Sierra Madre Occidental during the fourteenth century, the trails led through increasingly perilous territory. By 1350, the Chalchihuites culture had fallen and the desert beyond Zacatecas became the domain of wandering Chichimecs. Tarascans wrested control of the copper trade from the city of Casas Grandes and depleted its power. The population rebelled, or panicked. After an internal revolt, workers moved into the temples. Hostile tribes burned the city in 1450.

Even weak links with the Aztec empire created strife in the Southwest. Warfare and famine spread to the settlements of the Rio Grande. Hostilities broke out among them and their nomadic neighbors on the Great Plains. After 150 years of prosperity, people living on the open plains picked up and moved, west to higher ground, back to the cliffs.

Daryl Abrahamson, from the Colville Reservation in Washington State, dances at Santo Domingo Pueblo on the Rio Grande. He and his family travel to the Southwest each year to participate in the round of summer festivals. Dances and trade fairs have served as meeting grounds for centuries.

Portrait of lean, dark winter seasons, the Pueblo dancer becomes the cold: animal horns and hide, evergreens, abundant shells and turquoise. The Buffalo Dance, adapted from the tribes of the Plains, assures luck in the hunt. Russell Sanchez, Christmas Day, San Ildefonso Pueblo, New Mexico.

Eyes downcast, lightly tapping the earth, the maiden summons rain and plentiful crops for the coming year. Her traditional turquoise necklaces, dress of cloud terraces, sprays of evergreen, and basket of feathers are magical offerings. Christmas Day, San Ildefonso Pueblo.

Wearing bright beads, red porcupine hair, and eagle feathers, a Fancy Dancer from the Great Plains competes at the annual Gallup Intertribal Ceremonial, Gallup, New Mexico.

A Buffalo Dancer
from San Juan
Pueblo wears
parrot and eagle
feathers and ka-
china mask with
a Sun God design
at her waist. San
Ildefonso Pueblo,
Eight Northern
Pueblo Craft Fair.

The Santa Clara
Pueblo Basket
Dancer expresses
the exuberance of
women's work in
the cycle of seed
planting and har-
vesting. She wears
turquoise inlaid
spondylus shell, a
Zuñi turquoise
bracelet, coral
strands, and a sil-
ver Hopi bracelet,
and carries in her
hand parrot and
eagle feathers.
San Ildefonso
Pueblo, Eight
Northern Pueblo
Craft Fair.

A Pueblo dancer impersonates the Man-Eagle god, lord of the sky. Costumed eagle warriors appear in the ancient art of the Southwest and Mesoamerica and danced in honor of Quetzalcoatl, the Feathered Serpent. The shared belief in a feathered deity must be as old as our longing to fly. San Ildefonso Pueblo, Eight Northern Pueblo Craft Fair.

Overleaf:

The Horned Serpent basks on volcanic rock. When angered, his thrashings cause earthquakes, landslides, and floods. Monster of waters, he plowed the riverbeds with his horns at the time of creation. The Horned Serpent plagues rivers and wells, from New Mexico to the Yucatán Peninsula. Perched on the same boulder, the eagle is patron of war. The eagle is sometimes a feathered serpent in disguise, a shape-changer whose powers transform battle into a ceremony of rain and fertility. Galisteo Basin, New Mexico.

The Humpbacked
Flute Player plays
on rocks through-
out the Southwest.
A central figure in
Hopi rituals and
myth, the little
deity is bringer of
corn seeds and
rain. Here, over
the shoulder of a
feathered warrior,
he charms the
round symbol
of the four
directions and a
horned snake.
Galisteo Basin.

Shield, spear, and helmet of the Morning Star, Venus, identify this figure as a warrior of supernatural dimensions, related to the Hopi kachina of sky, clouds, and rain and to the Mesoamerican god Quetzalcoatl. The hero offers a clue to the hostilities threatening the Pueblos around 1400. The petroglyphs that run along the volcanic spine of Comanche Gap are an indelible record of the ceremonial life and history of the Pueblos who occupied the Galisteo Basin, south of Santa Fé, for three hundred years before they were driven out by raiders from the Plains.

A mock battle between Plains and Nambe Pueblo dancers captures the fierce vitality of the warriors of the sun. Past enemies, they come together during summer festivals. San Ildefonso Pueblo, Eight Northern Pueblo Craft Fair.

Stars and stripes on a dancer's mocassin reflect the complex loyalties of Pueblos and Navajos, who are members of nations within a larger nation. Gallup Intertribal Ceremonial.

Southern Fancy
Dancer. Gallup
Intertribal
Ceremonial.

AMERICA

give me a color
to step in,
a color for my
table, a color to
 thrash
my hands in—
my inner swirls
are grey with yes-
terday's promises
becoming today's
 raining wail.
        —Wendy Rose
          Hopi/Miwok

Mixing styles from many cultures, this dancer wears necklaces of Navajo and Santa Domingo origin, bone of Plains design, and eagle feathers and colored chicken fluffs.

Steeped in darkness, a San Carlos Apache performs the Crown Dance, the Venus war motif emblazoned on his chest, the American eagle and the Native American eagle warrior motif fused on his elaborate headdress. Apache bands ranged across the Plains and northern Mexico. Under visionary warriors like Geronimo, they withstood the U.S. cavalry, holing up in the Chiricahua Mountains, until their final defeat in 1900. Gallup Intertribal Ceremonial.

Feathers, pine sprigs, fringe, and feathers adorn a Navajo woman's prayer sticks. Feathers carry her prayers. New Mexico State Fair, Albuquerque.

The Women's War Dance celebrates the subtle art of the warrior and the unwaivering strength of the warrior's support. San Ildefonso Pueblo, Eight Northern Pueblo Craft Fair.

Drum of thunder, drum of time, drum of memory, drum of silent heart. Gallup Ceremonial Pow-Wow, Church Rock, New Mexico.

Left and opposite:

Fancy Dancers compete late into the night. Navajo Nation Fair, Window Rock, Arizona.

Plains warrior crouches behind his shield during mock War Dance. San Ildefonso Pueblo, Eight Northern Pueblo Craft Fair.

Praying hands of
hunters, warriors,
guard the sun,
heal the sick,
spear the stone
with lightning.
Black lava blooms
with moss and
lichen. Rattle-
snakes and lizards
draw birds down
from the sky.
Galisteo Basin.

Hands dusted with sacred corn meal, Pilar Aguilar of San Ildefonso Pueblo sweeps the earth in motion.

White Buffalo Woman gave the buffalo as a gift to the people of the Plains. The Buffalo Maiden blesses the hunt, long after thundering herds have vanished and a way of life was stolen. San Ildefonso Pueblo.

Overleaf:

Women pad in soft white mocassins, feet barely leaving the ground, bells jangling, the men bearing evergreen branches and shaking seed rattles, a long slow line in twos, repeating over and over, tap-tap, tiny steps, praising the earth, over and over. Women Basket Dancers and Deer Dancers from San Juan Peublo. Gallup Intertribal Ceremonial.

Turquoise, pine, rattle, bells, summer, winter, young men, old men. Turquoise, pine, rattle, bells. San Ildefonso Pueblo, Eight Northern Pueblo Craft Fair.

Buffalo Boy starting off, armed with rainbow and lightning. San Ildefonso Pueblo, Eight Northern Pueblo Craft Fair.

Under the ice,
under the snow,
the underworld
below is green
with summer and
the corn climbs
up to the sky.
Christmas Eve,
Nambe Pueblo,
New Mexico.

CHAPTER 3

THE SNAKE,
THE STONE, AND THE
SIX DIRECTIONS

Now in those days—much like today—there were people who traded stories. They were a poor lot, fit for nothing in this world but tireless talk and infinite silence. Everything on earth caught their interest. They were capable of interpreting the transits of planets and communing with the souls of moths. Inhabitants of supernatural worlds were as familiar to them as their next-door neighbors. They were just as skilled at spying on strangers, eavesdropping on the most intimate conversations without anyone taking notice. They had the gift of seeing at least four sides to every story, the good, the bad, the chaotic surface, and the buried heart.

There were wanderers who sang the deeds of divine kings, sages who traveled to the dwelling places of the gods and brought home luminous accounts of turquoise mountains, crystal rivers, and the jewels that adorned the goddesses. There were scores of heroic brothers who roamed the earth slaying monsters and returned with bones, colored stones, kernels of corn, or a bride to prove their story. There were people who never went anywhere and still had plenty to say: old men who remembered the beginnings of the world and old women who prophesied the end, hermits who filled the foggy air with plotless yarns and pointless dreams, seers who predicted instant success or catastrophe from their readings of dried beans.

There were maidens who translated the sighs of blossoms. Under the trees, in the middle of markets, along the roadsides leading away from river towns sat innumerable listeners, blessed with patience and time enough to hear the laments of passersby and repeat their tales of losses in tones of evening bells. Long ago there were stones that talked, birds that preached, dogs that conversed on the important issues of the day, and people who paid attention to their every word.

When people despaired of one another, stories gave them faith in animalkind: eagles that carried prayers to the sun, birds that dove below the waters and delivered messages from the gods of rain, rats and moles eager to answer polite requests, giant fish that gulped men whole and then spewed them out renewed, yellow dogs that paddled the dead across the underworld river. People spoke of lakes of sympathetic tears, mountains that defended towns from demons, trees that walked, stars that were once beautiful young men, and stones that climbed on top of one another and agreed to house the sky. Stories of a flood that destroyed the world captured everybody's imagination, from British Columbia to Peru, and served as a warning. Stories about the time before creation, and how the four worlds came to be, centered people's spirits. To everyone's delight there were thousands of stories about rabbits, ravens, and coyotes who played end-

Rabbit and moon, Mimbres

less tricks on gods and men. And when everyone gathered closer, there were astonishing stories of the moon that lit the telling of those stories.

In return for a laugh or a moral, people sometimes traded chocolate, beans, a bolt of cotton, a dozen turquoise beads—depending on the quality and flavor of the tale and, of course, the passion and humor of the storyteller. A sigh, a single exclamation, or a long silence was the usual reward for revelation. Little value was placed on glaring originality; audiences prefered familiar truths, unless new lies would serve them better. Although short stories became the rage for a while, people, as a rule, distrusted brevity. Sagas that unraveled over many nights, especially those spun out during ceremonies, won the most serious hearing and the highest praise.

Stories were beyond price, because stories have no end. Passed on from generation to generation, people still are singing and dancing to them and repeating them as they do their chores. Their plots guide every action and their words beat with the rhythm of the heart. They are the stuff of daily drama and the substance of dreams. They are free and they will last forever.

It is impossible to know when those words began, or whether the stories told today are whole or fragments or echoes. A few of the oldest narratives are recorded in hieroglyphic inscriptions, others

are preserved in black script or as disembodied speech on tape cassettes. Portraits of mythic protagonists survive in painted murals, on the surfaces of pots, hides, and boulders, in monumental sculpture, and in silver and turquoise ornaments. This divine cast of gods and heroes rises up to dance in the year-round cycle of celebrations. Stories come true.

Similar themes, characters, and motifs appear in growing variations told in dozens of native languages from Arizona to southern Mexico. Spread by word of mouth, translated, embellished, and recomposed over time and space, they belong to people who do not know one another and yet share a common vision. Some of the stories retold in this chapter are revised versions of tales that have appeared in print; others were recounted orally, and here are polished, sometimes embroidered, and occasionally reduced from thousands of words to mere distillations. Lost are the repetitions and responses, the sound of flute and drum, and the song.

Whether they reflect the wisdom of a solitary creator or generations of anonymous tellers, stories are the well of New World cultures, source of drama, dance, music, poetry, ritual, prayer, and healing. The mysteries of language and the arts, Native Americans say, sprang from the blue serpent, and if no one dares to assume his voice, every storyteller traces his winding path.

Now it still ripples, now it still murmurs,
ripples, still sighs, still hums,
and it is empty under the sky.
Whatever might be is simply not there;
only the pooled water, only the calm sea,
only murmurs, ripples, in the dark, in the night.
—Popol Vuh

Lord of lightning, rain, death, and rebirth, the serpent destroys and heals. Hopi Snake Priests draw on its powers during days and nights of fasting and prayers. When they emerge from the kiva they dance with tamed rattlesnakes in their mouths; afterward, the snakes are released to deliver messages to underground springs. Photographed at Walpi by Ben Wittick, 1887.

THE BEGINNING OF NEWNESS

Before the beginning of the new world, there was nothing throughout the great space of the ages save blackness and desolation. Only Awonawilona, the Maker and Container of All, had being.

In the Beginning Awonawilona thought, and from his thoughts mists grew and swelled. He made himself in the form of the Sun. With the first brightness of light, great clouds thickened and fell as water in water and the world-holding sea.

The Sun Father rubbed his skin and from his cuticles he formed the seed of the two worlds, impregnating the great waters. In the heat of his light the waters of the sea grew green and scum rose upon them, waxing wide and mighty until they became Awitelin Tsita, the Fourfold Containing Mother Earth, and Apoyan Ta'chu, the All-covering Father Sky. From their union upon the waters all beings—men, women, and creatures—were conceived in the fourfold womb of the world.

Now like all surpassing beings the earth mother and the sky father were as changeable as smoke in the wind, manifesting themselves in any form at will, as dancers do when they wear masks.

"Behold," said the earth mother as a great terraced bowl appeared within the water. "Upon me shall rest the homes of my little children. On the rim of each country terraced mountains shall stand." Then she spat on the water and stirred it with her fingers. Foam formed and gathered about the terraced rim, mounting higher and higher. "From my bosom they shall draw nourishment," she said. With her warm breath she blew across the terraces, white flecks of foam broke away, and floating out over the water were shattered by the cold breath of the father and the water of life descended to earth as fine mist and spray.

Then the father spread his palm and into the wrinkles and crevices he set seven yellow grains of corn. In the dawn of the early world they gleamed like sparks of fire. "When the terraces are dark, our children shall be guided by the stars of the six regions of space turning round the middle place, where our children shall live. Even as these grains gleam, so shall numberless seed grains like them spring up from the bosom of the earth when touched by my waters, to nourish our children."

Thus and in other ways they devised many things for their offspring.

—*Zuñi Creation Story*
after a translation by Frank Hamilton Cushing

Eagles and Eagle Dancers circled the hills of the School of Indian Lore, founded by naturalist Ernest Thompson Seton outside Santa Fé. Photograph by Harold Kellogg, 1931.

A SONG FROM RED ANT WAY

From deep under the earth they're starting off
the old men under the earth are starting off
they're decorated with red wheels and
    starting off
they're decorated with red feathers and
    starting off
at the center of the cone-shaped house they're
    starting off
because I gave them a beautiful red stone they're
    starting off
when someone does the same for me I'll walk the
    earth like them
on the red road they're starting off
from deep under the earth they're starting off

—Navajo
translated by Harry Hojer
with workings by Jerome Rothenberg

THE ANIMAL GUARDIANS

In ancient times, all beings on earth lived together in the City of the Mists at the center of the world. Posha-an-k'ia, god of the medicine orders, lived among his followers in human form. He taught the ancestors agriculture and the arts, introduced prayer sticks as a means of worship, and organized the holy medicine bands. Then he went into the world and divided the universe into six regions. In each region lay a great sea and in the center of each sea rose a sacred mountain peak. He placed his warriors, the prey gods, as guardians of the six world quarters and then vanished under the world, where he remains ruler and "maker of the path of life."

Yellow Mountain Lion is guardian of the north.
Blue Coyote is guardian of the west.
Red Badger is guardian of the south.
White Wolf is guardian of the east.
Eagle is master of the speckled upper world.
Mole is master of the black lower world.

These warriors deliver prayers to the gods and serve as mediators. As animals of prey they possess strengths that overwhelm other game. Fetishes of the prey gods, though made of stone, are believed to contain the breath of life in their hearts, the source of their magic powers. When carried during the hunt, they charm and weaken the victim. They also are effective in curing diseases.

—from Zuñi Fetishes

THE FIFTH SUN

The first sun, the watery sun, was carried off by the flood. All that lived in the world became fish.

The second sun was devoured by jaguars.

The third sun was destroyed by a fiery rain that set people ablaze.

The fourth sun, the wind sun, was wiped out by storm. People turned into monkeys.

The gods became thoughtful and got together in Teotihuacán. "Who will take on the job of dawning?"

Lord of Shells, famous for his strength and beauty, stepped forward. "I'll be the sun," he said.

Everybody looked at the Small Syphilitic God, the ugliest and wretchedest of gods, and said, "You."

Lord of Shells and the Small Syphilitic God withdrew to the hills that are now the pyramid of the sun and the moon. They fasted and meditated.

The gods made a bonfire. The Small Syphilitic God ran and threw himself into the flames. Immediately he emerged, incandescent, in the sky.

The Lord of Shells hesitated. Finally the gods had to push him in. Finally he rose into the sky. The gods were furious and beat him with a rabbit, until they extinguished his glow. Thus, the arrogant Lord of Shells became the moon. The stains on the moon are the scars from his beating.

But the resplendant sun didn't move. The obsidian hawk flew toward him. "Why don't you get going?"

The despised, purulent, humpbacked crippled one answered, "because I need blood and power."

This fifth sun is the sun that moves, gave light to the Toltecs and gives it to the Aztecs. He has claws and feeds on human hearts.

—Aztec
translated by Eduardo Calvino

LORD OF TURQUOISE

The Old Fire God sits at the core of the world, his heart smoking. When he burns, mountains quake. His words are rivers of fire. But what if he died? What would people eat? Cold would live in the

Temple with symbols of gold and turquoise, Mixtec codex

houses, nights black as ashes. Sly old man, all skin and bones and embers waiting to be fanned.

Lord of Turquoise among the Aztecs, he watched the sky. He kept his finger on the sun. He held earth's treasures in his hand and wore the finest turquoise earspools and pendants. His shield was green mosaic. He was kind to little children who had pierced their ears. He made sure merchants arrived on time. He presided over fire renewal ceremonies, rites of purification, soul cleansing, trials by fire. His flaming pathway led Aztec spirits toward sublime good fortune.

Turquoise talismans, the Navajos believe, bring good fortune and insure the favor of the gods. They are potent in affairs of the heart. Turquoise protects the wearer against contagious diseases. Turquoise is an emblem of the medicine man's powers.

The Hopis believe turquoise brings good luck in the hunt. Among the Apaches, a small turquoise bead attached to gun or bow makes the weapon shoot accurately.

Thrown into a river with a prayer to the rain god, turquoise is supposed to induce rain. Turquoise may be found at the end of the rainbow by searching in the damp earth. Turquoise is said to have stolen its color from the sky.

Among the Hopis, turquoises are believed to be the excrement of lizards.

—from Turquois

Lizard, Mimbres

HOW THE SUN STOLE TURQUOISES FROM CHIEF MORNING GREEN

One day long ago the women of Casa Grande were playing an ancient game called toka. While they were playing, a blue-tailed lizard fell from the sky. This wondrous event was reported to Morning Green, the chief of Casa Grande. Immediately he ordered the men to dig in the place where the lizard had landed. There they discovered a wealth of turquoises, which Morning Green distributed freely among his people. With the green stones they made many beautiful turquoise mosaics.

Soon the fame of these turquoises reached the ears of the Sun in the East. He sent the bird with bright plumage to steal them. When Parrot flew down to Casa Grande he was met by one of the daughters of the chief, who ran home and announced the arrival of a visitor from the Sun. Her father gave her a small stick and told her, "Take this charmed stick and when Parrot puts the stick in his mouth lead him to me." But Parrot was not charmed by the stick. The chief suggested that perhaps the strange bird would eat pumpkin seed. His daughter tried but Parrot refused. Her father suggested watermelon seed. Parrot was not tempted by these, nor by seed of cat's claw, nor was he charmed by charcoal, which, made of fire, is the most powerful magic in healing disease.

The chief of Casa Grande then told his daughter to give the bird some cooked corn served in a new food bowl. Parrot would not taste it, but noticing a turquoise bead of blue-green color, he gulped it down. The daughters of the chief immediately brought him some blue stones, which the bird greedily devoured. Then the girls offered a handful of the rarest turquoise beads. Parrot promptly ate them and flew away. As soon as he reached the home of the Sun in the East, he vomited his turquoises, which the sun god gave as a gift to the people who live near his house of rising beyond the eastern mountains. That is the reason, it is said, why these people have so many ornaments made of turquoise.

—*Pima*
after J. Walter Fewkes in Turquois

Quetzalcoatl, Lord of Wind, Mixtec codex

WIND COMES FORTH FROM FIRE

The Winter Corn Dances, held by the Pueblos after the annual fire renewal ceremony, summon wind and rain. The women's tall headdresses, crowns of stepped cloud terraces, are painted a vivid turquoise blue. At the center of each *tablita* is an open T, symbol of wind.

The trail of the wind symbol runs south. In the ruins of Izapa, on the Pacific coast of Chiapas, stands the oldest monument of the god of wind, Lord Ik. His symbol was the T. In time he blew the breath of life into God K, Maya lord of wind, rain, and lightning, whose symbol also was the T. The T-sign became the hieroglyph "Ik," the Maya word for wind, breath, and spirit. At Palenque, breezes flow through T-shaped windows, a symbolic architectural feature expanded three centuries later in the T-shaped doorways at Casas Grandes, Chaco Canyon, and Mesa Verde.

When hard winds prevail in the Southwest, the Pueblos offer turquoise stones to the wind spirit, to appease his anger so that the wind will stop and the rains begin. The Pueblos say that when the wind is blowing it is searching for turquoises.

HOUSE OF NIGHT

Spider Woman wove the Path of Souls, the Milky Way, which ran between the fingers of her hands. Then she made the Seven Grains of Corn, the Pleiades. She gathered up three threads and braided Three Loaves of Bread (Orion's Belt). She picked up two and cradled the Hero Twins, Monster Slayer and Born for Water (Castor and Pollux). Then she wound a huge knot and made the Big Star, Venus. The night sky is her loom. Her spindle whorls are made of turquoise.

Spider Woman taught the string game to Navajo women. With it they teach their children the constellations.

The Maya night sky is the house of life. Three stars of Orion's right thigh form the three Hearthstones of Creation. From the smoke of the woman's cooking fire the world is born.

The Pleiades are seven grains of corn. When planted below the horizon they grow into the Tree of Life, stretching across the enormous blackness as the Milky Way. Down the long hollow of the Tree runs the pathway to the underworld.

—from night talk in Chamula with Linda Schele
2 Muk'ta Sak, eve of the Maya New Year, 1992.

CALLING THE MOON

Turquoise Boy brought from the underworld a long reed with twelve holes. He lives inside the sun, and when he plays a note on his flute, the earth moves, month to month: moon of the parting-of-the-seasons, time of slender winds, moon of the great wind, ice moon, lizard belly cut moon, moon when eaglets chirp, month of little leaves, moon of the All-Wise Fly, dark leaf month, horse month, light ripening, moon when all is gathered in.

The symbol of the Moon Maiden, most beautiful of women, is a perfect ear of white corn wrapped in a cloud of snow-white feathers and adorned with ornaments of silver and turquoise.

SUN DAGGER

Our people found the stones and boulders that let in light. At Chaco Canyon a crevice in the cliffs opens for a sliver. The Sun Priests drew a spiral there and on the summer solstice the sun slices that rock in two. So, all it takes is light and a rock to tell the time of year. All it takes to count the moon are your fingers, counting the thumb twice in summer. The moon, the stars, the trees, the plants, the animals remind you. The mountains won't let you forget. The birds wake you. If you need to be someplace, I'll shake you.   —*The Town Crier of Walpi*

THE FEATHERED SERPENT

Quetzalcoatl, the Feathered Serpent, possesses the fangs, forked tongue, and trunk of a great snake. Instead of scales he wears the iridescent plumage of the quetzal bird. Unlike the Fire Serpent, the Feathered Serpent wears no crown. Although he is ubiquitous in the arts of Mesoamerica and still plays a dramatic role in rituals in Mexico and the Southwest, there are no descriptions of either earthly or supernatural sightings of serpents with feathers. On the other hand, ornithologists fortunate enough to have caught a glimpse of the delicate, near extinct quetzal in the last jungle sanctuaries of Chiapas and Guatemala, report that the trogon's long green tail feathers wavering through the forest canopy resemble the liquid movements of a flying serpent.

Far from the rainforest, the Feathered Serpent sometimes dresses in the plumage of the raven or the eagle. Free of feathers, his diamond markings form the pattern of the universe. His rattle whips the constellations. In human shape, Quetzalcoatl is the maker of life, bringer of corn, consummate artist, craftsman, and man of letters, the high priest of his religion, culture hero, and messiah. The Plumed Serpent in D. H. Lawrence's famous novel experiences a midnight conversion into a symbol of sexual potency, curiously tame, foolish, and constricted—misunderstood—in his Freudian cage.

The Feathered Serpent, like other supernatural snakes in the Southwest, is bound to earthly duties. Navajo chants sing of heroic battles with serpents, marriages to serpent brides, and serpent goddesses of the earth. The Great Snake, like his Mexican twin, is lord of lightning, rain, and wind. The Snake Dance at Hopi, in which the Snake Priests dance with rattlesnakes in their mouths, is the most daring display of union with the snake's powers of healing. The serpent of the Pueblos possesses the qualities of the universal snake: fertile, fierce, eternally changing.

Portraits of Quetzalcoatl in Southwestern rock art show him slightly bemused under a pointed cap,

**Feathered Serpent,
Teotihuacán**

Horned Serpent, Mimbres

THE HORNED SERPENT

The Horned Serpent is a Plumed Serpent with horns, or so he is depicted on the columns at the entrance to the Temple of the Warriors at Chichén Itzá. In the rock art of the Southwest the Horned Serpent wears a checkered neckband rather than a ruff. Among Nahuatl speakers, he is, quite simply, a deer snake.

Horned serpents continue to trouble the waters of the Southwest and churn beneath the landscape of Sinaloa, Veracruz, Oaxaca, and southern Mexico. The Zinacantecs of Chiapas make offerings to the Horned Serpent during well-cleaning ceremonies on Holy Cross Day.

Soon after the Hopis emerged from the underworld they were overwhelmed by a great flood of water rushing from the ground. The chiefs made two balls of powdered turquoise and shell which they offered to the water serpent who had caused the deluge. Immediately he was appeased and the water dried.

Horns, whether on snakes, deer, or antelope, in and of themselves contain magic. Members of the Two Horn Society at Hopi are among the most powerful medicine men. One Horn and Two Horn Priests are prominent ritual figures in the art of West Mexico. Among the Aztecs, the Two Horned God was the lord of duality.

the same distinguishing blue hat he wore among the Toltecs and the Huastecs. Along with his hat he carries the symbol of the morning star. On his journey up the Rio Grande he shared his attributes with several gods. The Heart of the Sky kachina, Sotuknangu, who controls lightning and torrential rains, wears a peaked hat and the symbol of the morning star. The Twin War gods bear the Venus emblem. Wherever he wanders, on the earth or in the sky, Quetzalcoatl is the god of transformation.

Big birds with long flowing hair and black clacking beaks, the Shalakos are rain spirits, warriors, and messengers who visit Zuñi in early December. Photograph by Ben Wittick, 1897.

HUMMINGBIRDS AND BATS

If you have ever watched hummingbirds battle, you know why Native Americans honor them as patrons of warriors and the *naguals* of powerful shamans. In Maya hieroglyphs the hummingbird represents invisibility, a supernatural trait attributed to some shamans and desirable among warriors. Tzintzuntzan, "Hummingbird," was the lyrical name of the capital of the Tarascans, famed for their featherwork, and unconquerable resistance to Aztec invasions. The hummingbird was the animal form of Huitzilopochtli, "One-Legged Hummingbird," Aztec god of the sun and god of war.

Blue hummingbird medicine man,
Come with me!
Yonder find my enemy
And make him helpless!

—*Papago War Song*
translated by Ruth Underhill

The hummingbird sometimes serves as messenger of the gods. Mainly he is a magician. He is capable of changing shape, changing color, and assuming the size of larger birds. He has been described as a white-winged dove and a sharp-shinned hawk.

At twilight, hummingbirds have a habit of turning into bats. Among the Zuñis, bats are respected guardians. The ancient Mimbres, like the Maya, associated bats with blood, death, and sacrifice.

The sanguinary, transformative duel between warrior hummingbirds and vampire bats brings rain.

When bats were at their fiercest they turned into jaguars. The Jaguar Bat, once common to Oaxaca, the Maya region, and Costa Rica, existed as the penultimate creature of night and the dark of the moon. Evidently it vanished sometime during the collapse of the Classic civilizations, for this monster is now extinct in folk memory. Carved in jade and cast in gold, its feline fangs and webbed wings still strike fear in the hearts of museumgoers.

114

Turquoise butterfly, Mixtec codex

TURQUOISE EYES

The Zuñi fetish of the Blue Coyote of the West is made of white limestone and has large turquoise eyes. The fetish is believed to possess the same qualities of intelligence, craftiness, and endurance by which coyotes dominate their prey. Coyote is a survivor.

A fetish carved in the shape of a sheep, with eyes inlaid with small turquoises, is supposed not only to secure fecundity of flocks, but also to guard against disease, wild animals, and accidental death.

Among the Keres of Santo Domingo Pueblo, a fetish of gypsum in the form of a prairie dog with eyes of turquoise is used to invoke the rain gods.

—*from* Turquois

LEARNING THE SPELLS

I am the beast she never knew or wished. I grieve
with lust: I will split her like the water's reeds.
That damp-backed woman's spell runs, wounded.
It hides, a coiled snake, under silken leaves.
Betrayal flies quietly on dark wings.

—*Anita Probst*
Yaqui

YELLOW BUTTERFLY

Among Native Americans, the butterfly is a great warrior. This story, told by anthropologist Alfonso Ortiz of San Juan Pueblo, explains the butterfly emblem seen in Mesoamerican art. The story, he believes, is one example of the Southwestern origin of a potent Mesoamerican symbol.

Listen. Two boys must meet the challenge of evil priests. They are completely helpless. They have no idea what to do. Then one of the boys sees a butterfly. They follow the butterfly to the Jemez Mountains in the west. There the yellow kachina is sleeping. He tells them he is the butterfly. From him they learn the arts of warfare. He gives them all the tools and weapons to battle the wicked priests.

The deer was a long time in the darkness.
He asked the spider to have a road made for him in the
   darkness.
Spider made the road and the deer's been traveling it.

—*from a Yuma Deer Dance Cycle*
Jerome Rothenberg's working, after Frances Densmore

RAIN CREATURES

"Mudheads" are rain creatures dredged from primordial ooze somewhere on the outskirts of Zuñi. Clowns, they have bumps for brains and their heads rattle with seeds and bits of yarn some crazy bird has stored in there. Even though their half-baked skulls sit on men's bodies, they are subhuman louts. They come at you, spitting obscenities. They drive you out of town and into nightmare. Then you discover they've been sleeping inside you all this time and your skin is the thinnest covering for a lizard waiting to crawl out and sun in the muck.

WINTER TALE

The red-winged blackbird was the handsomest boy in his village. From dawn to dusk he went about singing and his melodious song drew all the girls to him. In the mountains lived a solitary woman. She heard the red-winged blackbird's song at dawn, in the afternoon when she bathed, and in the evening as she sat by her fire. Then she heard his voice late at night and long before sunrise. His song had entered her heart. That year the gods sent perfect rains and the forest bloomed with the rarest wildflowers. She sighed, and the red-winged blackbird happened by and asked if she'd like to go walking. She said no, for he was a blackbird and she was the wind. He came the next day and the next. His song was so stirring the mountains and lakes started floating away. In her dream that night he said he was leaving. He promised to return before the next rains. "Take me with you," she said in her dream. Left on her bed was a blue turquoise beetle, which hastens the thunder of spring, though now the air was so empty only black leaves were flying.

—*Ramona Lee*
Taos

No longer the drifting
and falling of wind,
your songs have changed.
They have
become thin willow whispers
that take us by the ankle
and tangle
us up with the red mesa stone…
that follow us down
to Winslow, to Sherman,
to Oakland—to the ends
of all the spokes
that leave earth's middle.

—*Wendy Rose*
from "Some Few Hopi Ancestors"

Masked dancers of the Night Chant, a sixteen-day curing ceremony which traces the paths of mythic heroes from initial confusion and loss to the restoration of harmony. Photograph by Frasher.

THE HUMPBACKED FLUTE PLAYER

Xochipilli was the Aztec god of flowers. Inebriate he took the form of a monkey. As Macuil Xochitl, Five Flower, he was god of music and dancing among the Toltecs, who introduced him to the Mixtecs and to the Maya. He was married to the goddess of love.

Kokopelli, the Hopi god of fertility, is the harbinger of spring. As Locust, he came up from the underworld at the time of emergence, carrying with him seeds of corn. The sound of his flute charmed the dark and when the earth opened for him he charmed the snakes and hidden wells. His music melts snow. He lies on his back, rolls over, leaps from rock to rock, and somewhere in mid-air changes to a little dancing man, a diminutive Pan, hair flying, penis erect, playing his gay tune. Bending under his burden of mist and clouds, he plays for the dry arroyos. Along the Rio Grande, the Pueblos call him the Humpbacked Flute Player and he answers: waves his stick and the wind stops, plays a few lewd notes and the sky rains down on the corn.

If he represents an ancient trader loaded down with goods, how scrupulous is the little deity in his dealings with the storms? And those honored merchants carrying untold blessings may not have been high-minded holy wretches, as the priest Sahagún reports, but how like their gods, acquainted with the pleasures of the sacred road, bearing transcendental flowers, music, and love tokens for forgotten ladies. How faint the theories and pious the tales—of traveling merchants and musical divinities.

HIDDEN LANGUAGE

The stone-faced woman grew stonier as she sat by her hearthstones cooking stone soup and waiting for her old man to come home from clearing the cornfield of stones. Finally he appeared at dawn, rocking on his feet, his eyes red as garnets, and his pockets weighted down. "Look," he said, "I found these beautiful blue stones by the side of the road. There are so many it took me all night to pick them up. I brought them to you as a present." The woman's eyes turned green as serpentine and with one stroke she crowned him on the head with her mano. "Lies," she said. For days his mouth was full of pebbles.

—"Shortie"
Navajo

117

THE GREAT GAMBLER

Giants and monsters still roamed the country. People were forced to move from place to place. No sooner would they settle down when some awful monster would appear and terrorize them, and they would have to move again, to places they had heard about where plenty of wild seeds grew. Eventually the people came to Chaco Canyon. There they built large stone houses, planted crops, and flourished.

These people brought with them a great wealth of turquoise beads, which they regarded as sacred. The most sacred object in their possession was a huge round turquoise, as tall as a man, with twelve bright feathers around it.

The chief of these people never stepped out in the sun. The Sun became jealous of this chief whom he had never seen and wanted the beads and the great turquoise for himself.

Near the house of the chief lived a woman who was so poor she ate only the seeds of the goosefoot. She was of the Mirage Stone Clan. The Sun visited this woman secretly, and she bore him a son.

The woman taught the boy to run great distances. He grew to be handsome and tall. But because his mother was poor and he had no father, people mocked him. So he was always sad and sorry for himself. One day his father lowered the rainbow to earth and raised the young man to his home.

The Sun had a great plan. He gave his son two turquoise earrings as clear and perfect as the sky. Then he taught his son the gambling songs, and also a chant for drawing people to himself.

When the boy returned to Chaco Canyon, he started to gamble. People tried to buy his turquoise earrings, but he would say, "If you win them, you can have them." Whenever he chanted, people came to him and gambled away their wealth. Soon he was called Nahwiilbiihi, the Great Gambler, or Nahwiil-biihi Dine'e, the Winner of Men. He won everything. He won men, women, and children for his slaves. They worked for him, building the huge houses at Chaco Canyon. He won the Male Rain, the Female Rain, the Rainbow, rivers, mountains, and all the earth. It only rained where he lived, and the rest of the world went dry. He had plenty of corn and flowers. He won the wife of the chief and then the chief himself, together with his prayer sticks and turquoise beads. Last of all, he played for the great round turquoise, and he won this too. Then the Sun came down and said, "Son, you may keep all you have won, but the great turquoise is mine." But the boy smiled at his father and said, "Now I will gamble with you!"

The Sun went home angry and he thought up another plan. On the mesa near Farmington lived another woman of the Mirage Stone Clan. The Sun visited her and soon she had a son. This boy also grew strong and tall and at last went to his father's home, where he learned the games. His sister shaped him into the exact twin of the Gambler.

The Gambler was so powerful that he could not be beaten without help. And so, the Sun told the second young man, "Make me an offering of a white shell basket filled with chips of precious stones. Offer it with a prayer and I will help you." Then he told the boy to make offerings to the Wind Spirit and to the animals who would help him.

The boy gave a buffalo robe to Bat, which Bat still wears. To Big Snake he gave a red stone and to Measuring Worm a piece of black jet. He gave Rat a gift of white shell. For mixed chips of stones the Wind Spirit would help him see the Gambler's mind.

Woodpecker joined the plan for a red stone, which he also still wears. Dark Wind and Cut Worm also agreed to help.

The young man was given two beautiful young women to bet against the Gambler. They were the daughters of First Talking God and Second Talking God. They dressed the young man exactly like the Gambler, from head to foot, and set out for the Gambler's house. On their way they met Mountain Rat. They gave him white beads to please him. Further along they met Owl, who wanted to be part of the plan. They gave him white beads too. To this day gamblers put beads in the nests of rats and owls to bring luck in the games.

On they went. Dark Wind blinded the Gambler's spies with a dust storm. Bat flew ahead to hide in the roof beams of the Gambler's house where the first game would be played.

The young man arrived at the house. The Gambler's wife smiled. The young man said to the Gambler, "Brother, I come for the great turquoise."

The Gambler brought out his basket of dice sticks and shook it. "First we will bet our wives," he said. The dice sticks game uses seven sticks that fall either white side up or black side up. "Throw your sticks high up to the roof," said the young man. The Gambler shook his basket and said, "Mine is white." But Bat caught the Gambler's white sticks and threw down the young man's black ones.

The Gambler cursed and threw again. "This time mine is black." But Bat caught the black sticks and threw the white ones down. "Ha, you lost with your own sticks," said the young man. The Gambler was afraid for the first time. But he doubled his bets and asked for the hoop and pole game.

In the hoop and pole game the players roll a ring down a track and race after it. As the ring stops rolling each player throws a stick and tries to make the ring fall on his stick. The young man threw the ring and the race was on. The Gambler ran ahead and threw his stick first. As all the people watched, the ring rolled over the Gambler's stick and fell on the young man's. Why? Because Big Snake was inside the ring holding his tail in his mouth.

Bat, Mimbres

The young man bet all he had won and brought out his rainbow-shaped stick for the third game. When thrown into the air the stick would land points down, then fall to one side or the other. High in the air the stick flew; Measuring Worm was inside it, and he would not let the stick fall on the Gambler's side. By now the Gambler was soaked in sweat.

Next came the ball game. They had to hit a ball through the door of a house. The young man swung his club at the ball. Rat was inside it. He bounced straight for the open door, and the Gambler lost the fourth game.

Next they played the guessing game. The Gambler drew a picture of one of the sacred beings he had won and he drew nine circles. "Now," he said, "tell me the meaning of my drawing."

Wind Spirit, who knows everything and sees everything, whispered the answer in the young man's ear. "That is Water Boy," said the young man. "He has four beautiful flowers in each hand. He guards the sacred water jars. The first four hold Male Rain—black, blue, yellow, and white. The next four hold mists and the Female Rain—black, blue, yellow, and white. The eighth holds the white female rain, the flowers, and the pollen as well." "And the last great jar?" asked the Gambler, pointing to the last circle of his picture. The last jar held all his magic. At that moment the white bird that held the Gambler's magic flew from the jar. The Gambler hung his head.

To win the next game the young man had to kick a stick at three different marks on the ground and then over the great house itself. This he did because Woodpecker was in his stick.

In the seventh game two sticks were planted in the ground. The men raced and grabbed the one they thought was planted loosely. The other could not be pulled up. The young man ran for the wrong stick. But he pulled it out easily because Cut Worm had cut it free. When the Gambler tried to pull up the other stick it wouldn't budge and he landed flat, because Dark Wind had caused roots to grow on it.

The two men bet everything they had on the last game, the rain, the Holy Beings, the Sacred Turquoise. "Now we will race. If I lose, you can kill me," said the Gambler.

They raced to a hill where a ruin now stands, circled it, and ran back four times. The young man passed him each time. The Gambler shot all his arrows, but he missed. Then the young man shot at him. He hit the Gambler in the leg, the back, the shoulder, and the head. The young man won. The people cheered and blew their flutes. "I lose everything," said the Gambler. "Kill me while I am still warm."

The young man raised his arm to strike the Gambler with his club, but at that moment the Sun spoke. "Don't kill him. He is also my son, and he has nothing left on earth."

The Sun threw down his dark bow and told the young man to put the Gambler on the string. He shot into the sky. As he rose he called back twice. "Long ago I died in the center of the earth. My spirit will return." A third time he spoke but his voice could not be heard.

Then the young man said to his father, "Father, the Sacred Turquoise is yours."

The Sun said, "Thank you. Let us send our children to Huerfano Mountain. Above the eight rings of the mountain there is a house. That mountain is the earth's heart and it will be home forever." Before the young man left with his wife he went to the Gambler's house and pointed to the circles on the wall. He ordered them to return to all parts of the world. "From you the people of the earth will have rain, clouds, and mist."

He found the people who had been the Gambler's slaves. They were weeping because they didn't know what would happen to them. "Now you may go back to your own countries," he said. That day all the people left Chaco Canyon. Some returned to their old homes. Some said, "We have always dreamed of a new country. We will go there."

Some people say that the Gambler's last word was "Adios" and that he returned as a Spaniard. They say the moon took pity on him and gave him livestock, great riches, and a new people to govern. From him, they say, the Spaniards increased and in time some came up from Mexico and built towns along the Rio Grande.

—*from* Between Sacred Mountains

The Sun father created two boys, who slew the beasts of prey with arrows of lightning and turned them into stone. Instead of harming men and women, the magic spirits of the beasts serve people as a charm in hunting animals and in "hunting" diseases. The bear is the original guardian of the West. Turquoise fetish, Zuñi. Arrowsmith Collection, Santa Fé.

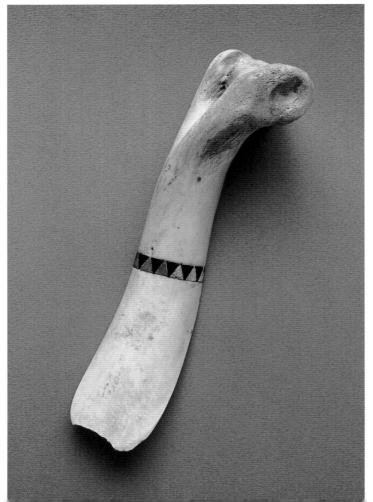
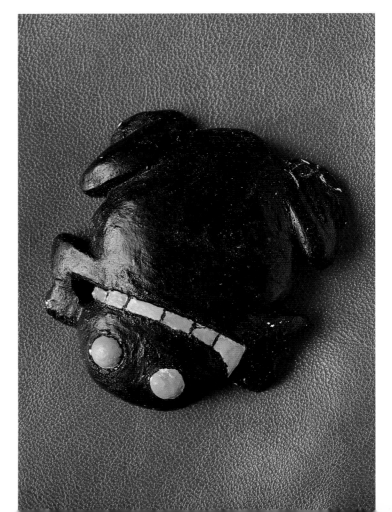

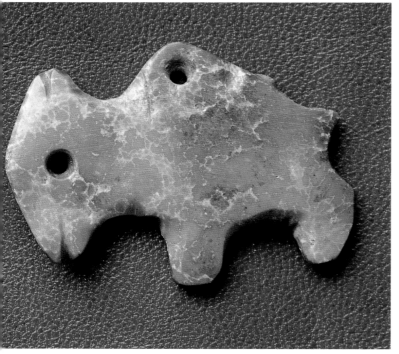

Opposite, clockwise from top left:

Frog pendant, turquoise. Mimbres, c. 1050. School of American Research Collection, Museum of New Mexico (27119/11).

Frog effigy, symbol of rain, carved spondylus shell with turquoise bead eyes. Zuñi, artist and date unknown. School of American Research Collection, Museum of New Mexico.

Facsimile of Anasazi frog effigy, jet inlaid with turquoise. Pueblo Bonito, Chaco Canyon, c. 1050–1300. Museum of Indian Arts and Cultures, Laboratory of Anthropology, Santa Fe (27359/11).

Facsimile of Anasazi ceremonial bone scraper, inlaid with turquoise and jet, found at Pueblo Bonito, Chaco Canyon, c. 1050–1300. Museum of Indian Arts and Cultures, Laboratory of Anthropology, Santa Fe (27360/11).

Above, clockwise from top left:

Pre-Columbian turquoise mosaic on stone. Museum of Northern Arizona, Flagstaff (A12379).

Turquoise mosaic surrounding bird of pink sandstone, found in northern Arizona. Pueblo III, c. 1100–1300; Museum of Northern Arizona, Flagstaff (NA700.B1.9).

Mimbres carved turquoise bison, c. 1050. School of American Research Collection, Museum of New Mexico (37407/11).

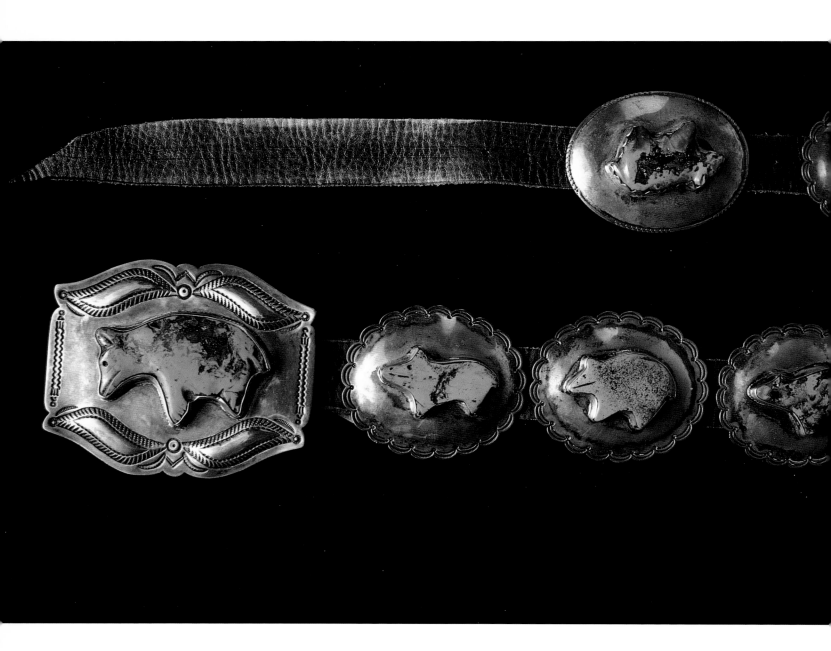

Above:

Bear fetishes carved by famed Zuñi artist Leekya Deysee animate this powerful *concha* belt. Derived from Spanish horse trappings, *conchas* ("shells") became a favored ornament among the Navajos. Since the turn of the century silver-smiths have used the hammered surface as a canvas to display precious turquoise stones. Turquoise from Beach Matrix Mine, Nevada.

Silver wrought by Roger Skeet, Navajo, 1942–43. C. G. Wallace Collection, Heard Museum Collection, Phoenix.

Opposite, above:

The frog and lizard, native creatures of the Southwest, grace two lively pins made for tourist trade. Frog: turquoise and centrifugal cast silver. Lizard: turquoise, coral, and ryolite inlaid in cast silver, Charles Loloma, c. 1920. School of American Research Collection, Museum of New Mexico

Opposite, below:

Icons of the American West, cattle are relative new-comers to the range, and to Native American jewelry. Left: Carved turquoise, red shell eyes, and fabricated silver bridle, horns, tips, and chain, Zuñi. Right: Turquoise eyes, bezel set, cast silver, Navajo. School of American Research Collection, Museum of New Mexico.

The ram assumes
the primordial
power of an
amulet on this
singular bracelet.
Turquoise, bezel
set, cast and
hand-forged
silver.

Silver canister displays the refined techniques of the jewelers' art applied to utilitarian objects. Bezel-set turquoise adorns the handle. Stamped, embossed, and forged silver. Artist unknown, c. 1960. Wheelwright Museum, Santa Fe (47/518 A&B).

Zuñi medallions, *conchas*, buttons, beads, and tassels decorate this lavish leather pouch. The lucky owner wears a Zuñi turquoise bracelet and Navajo *concha* belt. Photographed at the Navajo Nation Fair, Window Rock, Arizona.

Spectators at the Navajo Nation Fair wear traditional Navajo belts, each oval *concha* separated by turquoise-studded "butterflies." Turquoise and silver buttons decorate the blouses of the women on the left.

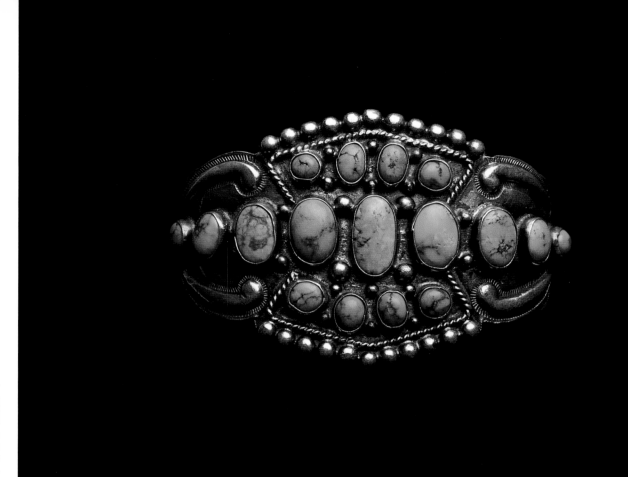

Turquoise bracelet, bezel set, twisted wire, and balls on embossed silver. Navajo, artist and date unknown. Wheelwright Museum, Santa Fé (47/389).

Hand-forged and stamped silver tobacco canteen. Turquoise, Navajo, artist and date unknown. Wheelwright Museum, Santa Fé (47/122).

Contemporary "needlepoint" bracelet, a technique developed by Zuñi artists about 1950. Dewey Jhahate, Apache, 1990. Turquoise from the Sleeping Beauty Mine, Arizona. Shiwi Trading Post, Zuñi, New Mexico.

Silver collar points were popular adornments between 1900 and 1950. Turquoise set in stamped silver. Navajo, artist unknown. Wheelwright Museum, Santa Fé (47/243A&B).

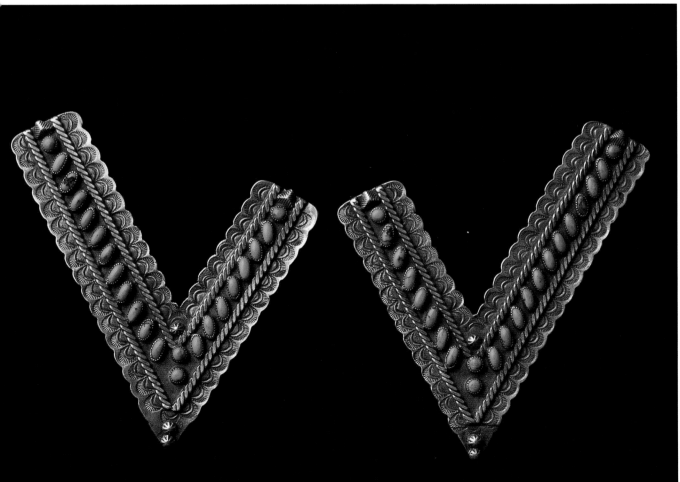

Overleaf:

Navajo woman wears matching Zuñi bracelets and matching Zuñi rings. Zuñi craftsmen prefer matching stones of even blue color, with little or no matrix. Each turquoise cabochon is individually bezel set in silver, framing a roseate cluster. Photographed at Indian Market, Santa Fé.

Surrounded by the tools of his trade—hammers, mandrels, wire cutters, jeweler's saw—Navajo silversmith Kee Joe Benaly chats at his bench as he begins soldering a new piece. Photographed in the emporium of Joe Tanner, Gallup, New Mexico.

Dennis Edaaki applies the final polish to a silver belt buckle with turquoise, jet, coral, and mother-of-pearl inlay. Photographed in his studio, Zuñi, New Mexico.

Carolyn Bobelu concentrates on an intricate inlay design. Photographed at home in her studio, Zuñi, New Mexico.

Sidney Hooee, a traditional Zuñi craftsman, chooses a stone for the delicate "petit point" necklace he is setting.

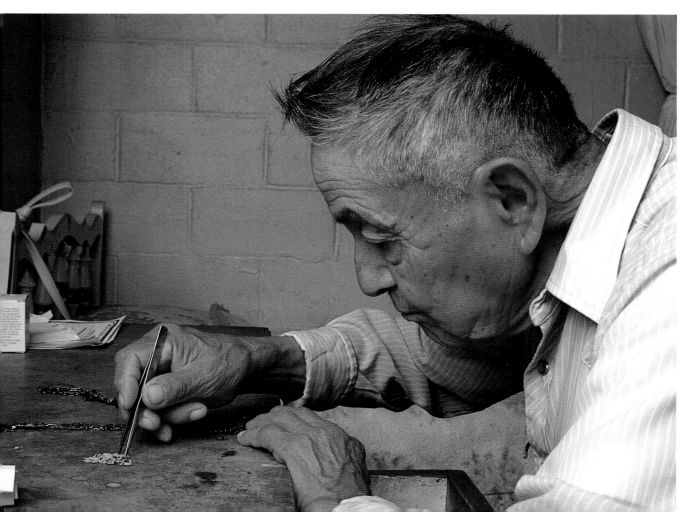

Sophisticated contemporary designs spring from ancient symbols and mosaic techniques in an evolving two-thousand-year-old craft tradition. "Arise in Beauty" pendant, channel inlay, Sleeping Beauty turquoise, Mediterranean coral, mother-of-pearl, and jet on gold. Carolyn Bobelu, Zuñi/Navajo, 1982. Artist's Heirloom Collection.

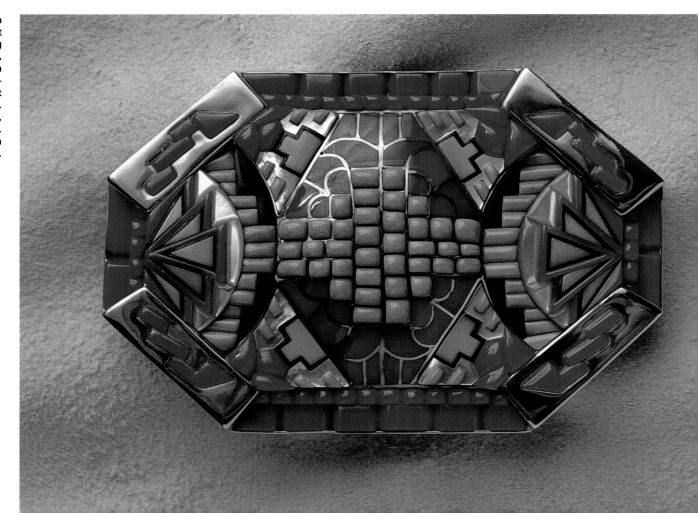

"Promise of a New Day" belt buckle, Sleeping Beauty turquoise, Mediterranean coral, mother-of-pearl, and jet inlaid in gold. Carolyn Bobelu, Zuñi/Navajo, 1985. Artist's Heirloom Collection.

Ketoh (bow guard), cast silver, spider-web turquoise from Timberline Mine, Nevada. Francis Jones, Navajo, 1974. Collection of Tom Woodard, Santa Fé.

Sandcast silver *ketoh* with turquoise. Probably Navajo, artist and date unknown. School of American Research Collection, Museum of New Mexico (SAR1986-1-4).

Zuñi elders display their wealth of turquoise finery; turquoise, they say, guarantees long life.

Right: Crystal Shekya wears examples of custom work from the 1960s: a squash blossom necklace with inlaid sun faces made by her daughter, and a matching Eagle Dancer bracelet and ring.

Opposite: Ella Pinto, 100 years old, is the oldest woman in Zuñi. Her jewelry dates back to the 1940s.

A bandolier of bone, turquoise, brass, and glass beads—a Plains design—is part of the Pueblo dancer's costume. San Ildefonso Pueblo.

This outstanding hishi necklace, created by John Christiansen, Sac and Fox, in 1989, is composed of fine turquoise, coral, jet, and gold beads, each bead less than 1/l6" in length. Strands of shells, and perhaps turquoise, were used as money in Pre-Columbian times. Tom Woodard Collection, Santa Fé.

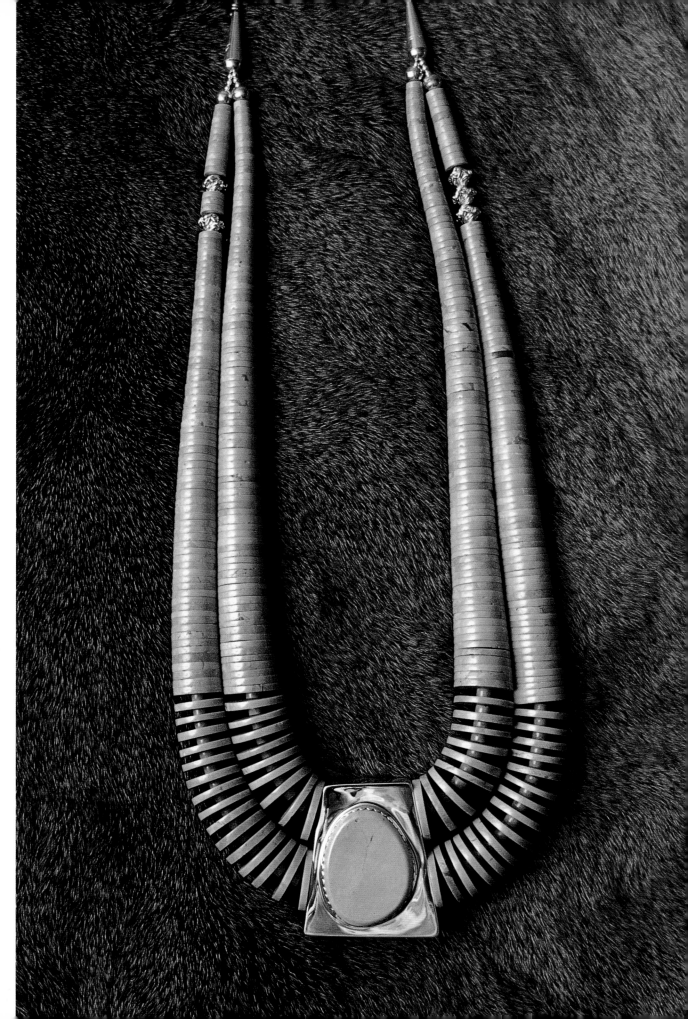

The traditional Jacla necklace of matched or graduated turquoise and spondylus shell beads has been prized by the Navajos for centuries. Before the Conquest, the strands were a popular trade item between the Navajos and the Pueblos of the Rio Grande.

This spontaneous interpretation of the bow guard, cast in hammered silver and set with turquoise and branch coral, is a 1950 work by famed Zuñi artists Dan Simplicio and Leo Poblano. Their rhythmic designs were influential during the 1930s. Tom Woodard Collection, Santa Fé.

Turquoise, coral, and brass knife handle by sculptor Charles Pratt, Arapaho/Cheyenne, cast in 1984. Tom Woodard Collection, Santa Fé.

French fleurs-de-lis distinguish this squash blossom necklace. Sandcast and stamped silver *naja* and blossoms, handwrought silver beads, and turquoise. Navajo, c. 1920–30s. Private Collection.

The bold use of large turquoise cabochons is characteristic of Navajo jewelry. Bracelet and squash blossom necklace of Morenci turquoise, bezel set, fabricated silver and handwrought silver beads, both by Mary Avery, Navajo, c. 1970. Bill Malone Collection, Ganado, Arizona.

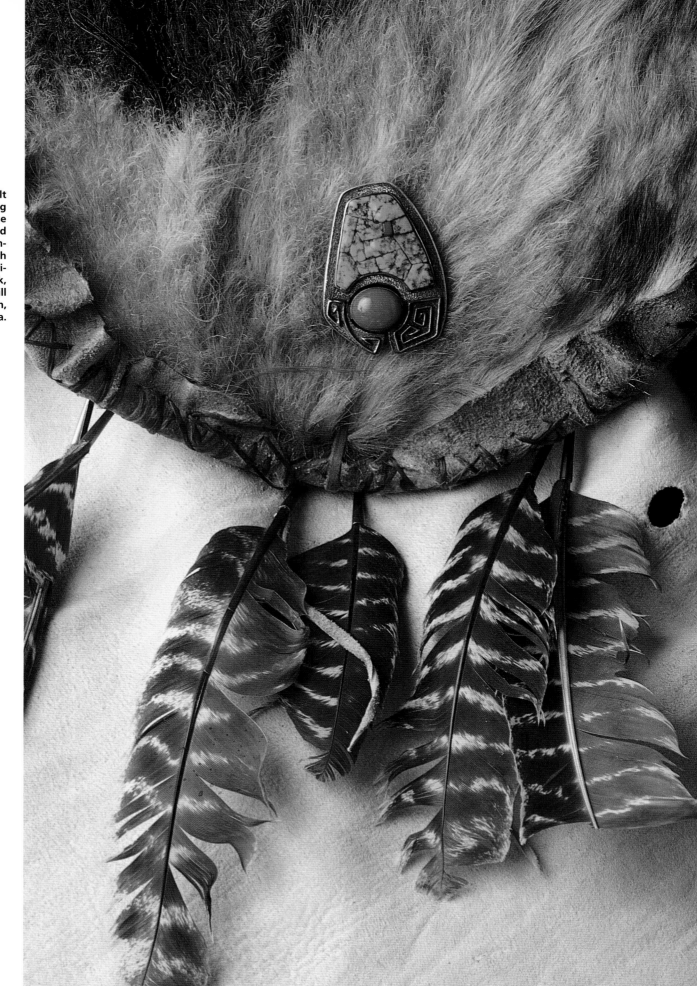

Contemporary belt buckle featuring Morenci turquoise nugget and round coral. Silver embellished with wire scroll, fabricated. Victor Beck, Navajo, c.1970. Bill Malone Collection, Ganado, Arizona.

Top: Hammered wire bracelet decorated with handwrought silver leaves and twisted wire and Morenci turquoise. Mary Avery, Navajo, c. 1970.
Middle: A row of distinctive Persian turquoises set on round wire bracelet. Percy Shorty, Navajo, 1987.
Bottom: Morenci turquoise and coral surrounded by petals on cast and hammered silver bracelet. Mary Avery, Navajo, c. 1970.
All pieces Bill Malone Collection, Ganado, Arizona.

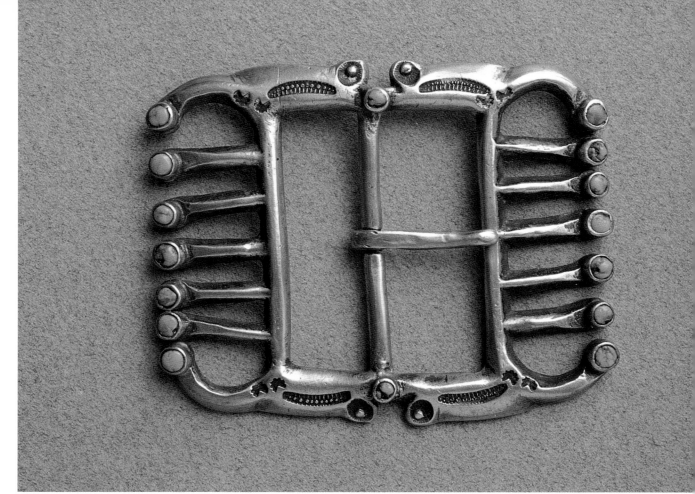

Raw simplicity adds power to this Navajo belt buckle. Turquoise and cast silver. Artist unknown, c. 1940. Millicent Rogers Museum, Taos (1980-17-327).

Early Navajo smiths melted down coins for silver; "coin" or "nickel" silver is heavier than sterling and contains about 20 percent less silver. Here, a Liberty Head silver dollar is the centerpiece for a bracelet, framed by twisted wire, stamped balls, and turquoise gemstones. Navajo, artist unknown, c. 1940. The piece was collected by heiress and socialite Millicent Rogers. Millicent Rogers Museum, Taos (1974-7-128).

Timepiece of
turquoise and
silver, Navajo
post-modern.
Photographed at
the old Hubbell
Trading Post,
Ganado, Arizona.

Keeper of the
Turquoise Trail.
Photographed
at the Navajo
Nation Fair,
Window Rock.

CHAPTER 4

THE LAND OF
DREAMS

Long ago and beyond the sea there lived in the land of Hispania a people with black beards and the legs of Arabian steeds. Their patron saint, Santiago, rode for God. In their blood ran strains of Berber horsemen, Celtic wanderers, Greek traders, and Roman gold miners. Centuries of living under the yoke of the Moors gave their temperaments a fatalistic cast, more brooding than the Italians, more practical than the Dutch, more romantic than the French, more pious than the Portuguese, and more zealous than the infidels.

Spaniards were born with an unslakable desire for immutable beauty. Spanish rulers pledged themselves to the pursuit of divine treasures, though they lay in the bosom of the Islamic Empire. Traders suffered the trials of Sinai to secure turquoises from the mines of the Egyptian goddess of the sky. Merchants of Aragon amassed Oriental silks, brocades, and velvets to drape the nobility in the most lavish veils of the spirit. Royal minters, as gifted as Vulcan, converted precious metals into slightly baser coins, the fluctuating weight of which they artfully disguised with images of angels, goddesses, and serpents. Bishops' vestments dazzled archangels. At the sight of loveliness the soul of the pettiest thief took wing. Spires of Spanish Gothic cathedrals rose like oaks toward the seventh heaven. Golden altars enveloped the most sanguine, transfixed Christs.

Medieval ecclesiastics regarded history as the manifestation of God's plan on earth. When the Crusades united human and divine destiny on the path to Jerusalem to fight the infidel, the brotherhoods of Spanish knights were among the most treacherous in battle. They murdered in the service of the ideal, disdaining the materialism of the merchants and the corruption of the clergy. Finally they were answerable to God's law, their actions weighed by justices who wrote briefs and pardons that extended to volumes of papyrus. They exacted the same verbose apologies from the guilty. Spaniards held in highest esteem the power of the word.

Hard realism vied with medieval mysticism in the tragic soul of Spain. Her most learned humanists surrendered to religious flights. The oriental vanity of her nobles rose to sobering heights; they failed to see themselves as mere mortals. Her conquistadors were brutal, brave, contemptuous, and willing to starve to achieve their goals. Their search for the extraordinary drove them on fantastic adventures, their striving for the infinite made endless voyages a spiritual pilgrimage. Honor, virtue, and romantic sensitivity lodged in a flawed, dreaming knight, Don Quixote. Heroes, in literature and in life, fell out of favor and out of step with the rest of the world, stumbling, culpable picaresques on impossible quests.

Reptile's eye, Teotihuacán

The quixotic also penetrated the realms of science and philosophy. The discovery of Aristotle's works challenged God's supreme role as master of creation and human destiny. Aristotle believed man's natural wisdom would guide him in shaping a more perfect society. Averröes, an Arab philosopher in the twelfth-century court of Córdoba, resolved the dilemma by proposing the existence of an intellectual soul, which united man's spiritual and rational propensities. The theory was reduced to the doctrine of "double truth," that reason and revelation were equally true, though completely incompatible. Long after the church denounced Averröes, the theory of the double truth prevailed. People knew from daily experience that faith and reason walked side by side, and that the world was full of phantasms as well as natural wonders. No science or sophistry could extinguish miracles and dreams.

Scholars pursued both avenues of truth simultaneously. The resulting mixture of the supernatural and rational, the spurious and scientific proved infectious. Aristotle, after all, having relied on observation to explain the workings of the universe, had concluded that the rivers of the world emanated from mountain caves and that migrating birds wintered at the bottom of the ocean.

Turning to the medical benefits of minerals, Aristotle noted that turquoise was effective in treating scorpion stings and epilepsy. King Alfonso the Wise composed a monumental treatise on precious stones that acknowledged man's bond with the mineral world. The great German scholar Albertus Magnus wrote an encyclopedic tome on the magical properties of gems, confessing that he stole his ideas from Aristotle. Turquoise, for example, was said to cure ailments of the head and heart, restore night vision, and ward off the evil eye. The stone helped clairvoyants see the future. Worn as a charm, turquoise promised good luck, health, and happiness. It captured the hearts of lovers and guaranteed victory over enemies. The mere sight of the gem could induce laughter. Associated with the cardinal directions, with the magic shield of Aaron, and with the Virgin Mary, turquoise assured sublime power over men and nature.

Of all things earthly, gold—"petrified sunlight" —was the supreme cure for body and soul and the symbol of social harmony. Yet gold was all too rare.

Men awaited the rebirth of the Golden Age, while alchemists searched for the eternal in nature. The quest for the philosopher's stone ultimately required spiritual transformation. The most outspoken practitioner, Theophrastus Paracelsus Bombast, Monarch of all the Arts, Prince of Philosophy and Medicine, acquired his knowledge of the transmutation of metals by studying the arcana of the Golden Age, and by observing iron smelters at work. As a physician, who spent his internship healing lead miners in the Tyrol, Paracelsus treated patients by prescribing sulphurs, salts, mineral baths, and rings of precious stones and metals. Disease, Paracelsus argued, resulted, not from vague humors, but from the imbalance of minerals in the body. The alchemical alteration of tin into silver or gold, Jupiter into Luna or Sol, figuratively combined the regenerative powers of heaven and earth. As the object of spiritual and material aspirations, gold represented the complete union of opposites.

The age reeled with the spirit of God while coveting gold, silver, and jewels that shone like the sun, moon, and planets. The gleam of gold, which would

Place of Seven Caves, Mixtec codex

make one rich beyond one's dreams, obsessed every soldier, priest, merchant, queen, cartographer, rogue, and man of reason. For to rise in the world was to rise in spirit. Divine rewards were plain. Through tireless dedication to opulence Spain achieved commercial domination over the Mediterranean and began to seek her fortune in the west. At the dawn of the new Golden Age the king of Spain, Carlos V, sat as supreme ruler of the Holy Roman Empire and fount of union for all of Europe. Spain was the leading power in the world.

Dramatic news that the sun rotated at the center of the universe was made palatable by the continued belief that God was the sun, and the sun was gold. As Spain set out to explore the world, the earth turned into a treasury, to discover, loot, and capture for the greater glory of God. Mountains may erode, rivers cease to flow, and all things slowly wear away. Gold alone never tarnished, would neither rust nor decay. Gold was the pure soul.

The ancient books of Plato contained a legend of a great continent in the west, Atlantis, which had sunk in a cataclysmic earthquake that left only a few lonely islands where gold lay in abundance. The Greeks also told of the Blessed Isles, beyond the Pillars of Hercules, where the souls of the dead voyaged. There, Plutarch wrote, slept Saturn, god of fecundity and ruler of the Golden Age.

The Danes spoke of the islands of Valhalla to the west, where their thunder god Wodin dwelled. The Irish believed that King Lir, god of the sea, was ruler of the western domain of death. For Arabs, the western ocean was an immense Sea of Darkness and Mystery, infested by krakens that ate men whole. The world, the Italians argued, was as round as a lemon that spun in a sea of emptiness round the sun. Nicholas of Cusa knew the earth was round because the earth was perfect and the perfect shape was the circle, whose center was God. Yet heaven above and the sea below were girt by a giant dragon that circled the world from Asia to Spain. On St. Brendan's voyage in search of the Isle of the Blest he saw great monsters, islands where the birds were fallen angels, fish fed on metal, and the sea a jeweled crystal temple.

The Spaniards were lured by the legend of the Seven Cities of Gold. It was said that a band of Christians under the last Visigothic ruler, King Roderick, had escaped to an island in the west during the Moorish invasion of the Iberian Peninsula in 711. The sands of the island shimmered with gold, and in the shelter of seven identical tri-lobed bays the Christians established seven cities: Aira, Ansalli, Ansodi, Con, Anhuib, Ansesseli, and Ansolli. The fabled cities, in another version of the story, were established by the archbishop of Portugal and six bishops who fled Iberia by ship in 737.

By the Late Middle Ages the island had multiplied like a sea creature, spawning from the northern Atlantic to the coast of Brazil, loosing gold dust on the waves. On medieval maps the rectangular island with its perfect bays floated freely over the ocean. The Island of the Seven Cities of Gold was the Canaries, then the Azores. Finally it came to settle off the coast of Florida and be called Antillia, a name derived either from the Arabic word for "dragon," or Lake Antela in Spain, source of the River Limia, water of oblivion. In the next century of exploration the Seven Cities of Gold drifted away to the dry sea of the American Southwest.

Among the thousand things sought by Christopher Columbus, son of a Genovese merchant, were the Seven Cities of Gold. He had acquired maps of Antillia from an Arab. And according to Las Casas, who spied Columbu's log, he had copied in his notebook the story of a ship that accidentally had landed on the isle in 1438, during the reign of the Infante D. Henrique. To their delight, the lost sailors were greeted by natives who spoke Portuguese. More happily, the crew discovered that the sands of the island contained grains of gold.

In the year that Spain drove out the Moors, Columbus set out on his epic voyage. For weeks he sailed the cobalt seas and never saw a dragon. When he reached the Sargasso Sea, Columbus calmly wrote, "The air is soft as April in Seville. It is a pleasure to be in it, so fragrant it is." He encountered no engulfing weeds, no maelstroms, no remoras. The little caravels did not drop off the rim of the world, nor did his men hear sirens sing. Instead they were dazed by the endless ocean. Wave after wave rocked them, and they soon thought of the sea as a cradle, and though their bodies ached with the pains and hunger of old age, they clung to illusions of youth and a perfect home beyond the horizon, and time shrank into an eternal golden phosphoresence wave after wave on the water. They were sailing slowly toward the gold of Paradise. When the cry came from the crow's nest, three of the crew believed they saw the royal barge of the Khan rowing out to greet them. The barge with its silk canopies blown by sylphs was a purple water hyacinth washing out from shore.

The island of Hispaniola, wrote Peter Martyr, was shaped like the leaf of a chestnut tree. Columbus sank to his knees and claimed a fertile land that would yield radishes, cabbages, and sugar within fifteen days of planting and cucumbers in thirty-six. He claimed the palm trees, the tuctuc birds nesting among the rocks, the men and women who came down to greet him at the shoreline, believing the Admiral had descended from the sky.

In return for little hawk bells the natives presented gold nuggets the size of stones. When the Admiral promised anything they asked for, the Indians promised nuggets of gold as big as walnuts, as big as oranges, as big as the head of a child. They simply had to pluck them from the rivers.

In Cuba the natives brought parrots, bread, and doves. An old man stepped up and caught the Admiral's ear. He reminded the Admiral that the souls of men may make two journeys, one down a road foul and dark, the other pleasant and delectable, depending on whether a man has been cruel or peaceful. Columbus politely thanked him for his views touching upon the journeys, rewards, and punishments of souls. He declared that he had come to discuss those very matters by order of Queen Isabella and King Ferdinand of Spain.

Tlaloc, god of rain, lord of paradise, Teotihuacán

In his letter to the king, Columbus described the islands in the Indian Sea as a wondrous paradise of beautiful mountains, salubrious rivers, and safe harbors, nightingales singing through winter and fruit trees reaching to the stars. The men and women, naked as the day they were born, already practiced the golden rule. "Mine and Thine have no place with them," wrote Peter Martyr. "They seem to live in the golden world, without toil....They deal truly one with another, without laws, without books, and without judges."

On successive voyages Columbus encountered Maya sea traders plying cargoes of copper bells, copper axes, cotton mantles, and cacao in huge canoes. He met Panamanians naked but for golden amulets. Nowhere did he discover great cities, palaces, or hoarded treasuries of gold. The natives seemed more savage and Paradise more elusive.

In Tenochtitlán, city of seven caves, a three-tongued fire bled like a wound in the sky. Lightning bolted from the sun. A gray heron with a round mirror glinting in its forehead flew into the snares of the royal huntsmen. Gazing into the mirror, Montezuma saw heaven and the stars and conquerors marching in war regalia. "What shall I do?" he asked. "Where shall I hide?"

His empire stretched east to the Gulf, west to the Pacific, and south to Guatemala. In the city "of amazement-breeding magnificence," Montezuma built temples for all the foreign gods of Mexico. People of every deformity danced before his court. His aviaries sang with parrots, toucans, hummingbirds, and quetzales. His zoo contained every creature of land and sea and his hanging gardens grew lush with every variety of flowering and healing plant. His smiths cast fish, birds, and butterflies in pure gold. A god, no one dared to look upon his face, no one had ever seen him eat. His feet had never touched bare ground.

Montezuma executed ten thousand dreamers who foretold the end of the empire. The soothsayers of the rival king of Texcoco prophesied destruction. King Nezahualpilli, certain that his soothsayers accurately predicted the future, challenged Montezuma to a ballgame, the outcome of which would confirm, once and for all, the powers of the royal seers. Montezuma lost the competition and fell into final despair. "If only I could turn into stone rather than suffer that which I so dread."

PROPHESY OF THE RETURN OF QUETZALCOATL

Eat, eat, while there is bread
Drink, drink, while there is water
A day comes when dust shall darken the air
When blight shall wither the land
When clouds shall arise,
When mountains shall be lifted,
When a strong man shall seize the city,
When ruin shall fall upon all things.
On that day, the tender leaf is destroyed,
On that day, the dying eyes are closed,
On that day, three signs are on the tree,
On that day, the battle flag is raised,
And they are scattered afar in the forests.

—Chilam Balam of Tizimin
translations by George Brinton
and Gordon Brotherton

When Hernan Cortés landed on the shores of Veracruz in 1519, emissaries of Montezuma welcomed Cortés with presents: a golden image of the sun, as big as a cartwheel, a wheel made of silver as dazzling as the moon, a helmet full of grains of gold, a golden menagerie of tigers, lions, monkeys, dogs, ducks, and deer, ten gold collars, two golden staffs of justice, crests of gold, plumes of rich green feathers, and, recounts Bernal Díaz, Cortés' chief lieutenant, "four *chalchihuites*, which are green stones of very great value...each one being esteemed more highly than a great load of gold."

The Spaniards picked up the gold and fingered it like monkeys, observed the Aztecs. "They seemed to be transported by joy, as if their hearts were illuminated and made new."

Cortés accepted these novelties and gave the chiefs a few beads of twisted glass and for Montezuma, a gold medal engraved with a figure of St. George on horseback slaying the dragon.

Aztec ambassadors dressed Cortés as Quetzalcoatl, in a mask of turquoise mosaic adorned with twisted snakes. They gave him Quetzalcoatl's staff of turquoise mosaic ending in a coiled serpent's head. They gave him the turquoise mask of Tezcatlipoca and the turquoise mask of Tlaloc. "Is this all?" asked Cortés. "Is this your gift of welcome? We Spaniards suffer from a strange disease only gold can cure."

The Spaniards offered Montezuma a stale sea biscuit which weighed more than a stone. This gift was borne to Tula and buried in a gold gourd in the temple of Quetzalcoatl, where it was worshipped as the food of the gods.

...and when we saw so many cities and villages built in the water and other great towns on dry land and that straight and level Causeway going towards Mexico, we were amazed and said that it was like the enchantments they tell of in the legend of Amadis, on account of the great towers and cues and buildings rising from the water, and all built of masonry.... Of all these wonders that I then beheld today all is overthrown and lost, nothing left standing.

—*Bernal Díaz del Castillo*

Encased in iron, the Spaniards rode from the sea and took the seat of empire. The din of horses' hooves shook the earth. "Before them ran their armored dogs," wrote Sahagún, "with foam dripping from their muzzles."

They marched south under great volcanoes, and the winds of the Strait of Tehuantepec drove hem on. Friars climbed the mountains on chairs strapped to the backs of Indians. They passed the ancient cities. They took to the rivers in ships.

When they reached Chiapas, Maya warriors threw themselves over the Sumidero Canyon rather

Quetzalcoatl, patron of the arts,
Mixtec codex

than surrender. Pine trees danced. The rain turned black.

The Spaniards kept on marching, into the cold highlands, into the torn jungles. The last rulers of the Itzá fled.

The Spaniards brought the true god, the Virgin of Sorrows, and the saints. The sister of the gods dragged herself along, covered with dust, covered with cobwebs. The Aztecs perished, their mouths dry as straw. They ate frogs and snakes.

Hernan Cortés, conqueror of the New World, melted down the golden treasures and shipped the ingots back to Spain.

I think that if I were to say to one of the Indian women who love to wander around the markets, "Listen, today is market day in such and such a place. Which will you choose, to go straight to heaven or to go to the market?" I suspect she would say, "Let me first see the market, and after that I will go to heaven."
—*Father Diego Durán*

The kingdoms of the New World delivered an abundance of things never before seen or known. Each year the Spaniards sent to Seville one hundred ships laden with gold, silver, copper, jades, pearls, and turquoises. Indian jugglers, acrobats, ballplayers, and dwarfs arrived to entertain the Spanish court. Apes and armadillos, jaguar skins, cotton, and cochineal came each day from the new-found world. Receiving the first pineapple, overripe

after six weeks at sea, King Carlos declared it the most heavenly fruit he had ever tasted. Besides love-apples, coffee, and chocolate, came tobacco, herbs, roots, juices, and stones whose great medicinal virtues were deemed more precious than temporal goods.

Sailors returned with tales of white-skinned, blue-eyed savages, a tribe of one-legged pygmies, women with two heads, and men with wings who flew like bats from tree to tree. Mariners told of icy kingdoms of gold and rubies, cities of gold, silver, and giant pearls, houses supported by pillars of crystal, and natives adorned with collars and bracelets of gold.

Having sacked the kingdoms south of the Valley of Mexico and still unsatisfied with the spoils, Cortés ordered reconnaissances of the Northern Mystery. Perhaps they would discover a shortcut to China and, on the way, a kingdom rumored to be rich in pearls and gold. Only one danger could befall them, the Tarascans warned: the land was ruled by Amazons who ate men.

Alvar Nuñez Cabeza de Vaca already was crossing the unknown. A commander of the ill-fated Narváez expedition of 1527, he had set out in search of the Seven Cities of Gold, when he was shipwrecked off the coast of Florida. The survivors stitched new sails of shirts, braided ropes of horsehair, and

**Mixtec shield,
gold with turquoise inlay**

sailed for Louisiana, where they were cast up on the Isle of Misfortune. Cabeza de Vaca and three companions, Alonso Castillo de Maldonado, Andrés Dorantes de Carasco, and Estevaníco, a black Moorish slave, walked west, across Texas, southern New Mexico, and Arizona, following the sun. For five years the Spaniards worked as slaves, surviving on oysters, prickly pears, grubs, and mesquite. Set free, de Vaca became a merchant, trading conch shells and beans for red ochre and flints. The Pimas gave him "emeralds shaped like arrowheads," green turquoises, malachite, or peridots which they had bought with parrot plumes from the Pueblos of the north.

On his epic journey toward the sun de Vaca acquired a mysterious gift for healing. He made the sign of the cross and the infirm came back to life. Wherever he traveled the Indians brought to him their sick and wounded. In return for his prayers the starving Indians gave him whatever food they had. De Vaca became a savior followed by processions of worshippers, the Children of the Sun.

As they neared the Pacific coast of Mexico, the naked band at last encountered a countryman: Nuño de Guzman, conqueror of Sinaloa and Nayarit, notorious murderer, and slave trader hunting down natives whose brother de Vaca had become. For eight long years de Vaca had lived as an Indian; the meeting left him bereft.

Following a triumphant welcome through the streets of Mexico City, de Vaca returned to Spain. He expected to receive, as his reward, a commission to lead an expedition to Florida and the Fountain of Youth. Instead, Spain sent him to South America. Within two years de Vaca was hacking his way through the jungle of Paraguay to Iguazu Falls. Only Estevaníco, the Moroccan slave, was willing to return to the north in search of the Seven Cities of Cíbola, which, the Indians had told him, contained an unimaginable wealth of gold.

Father Marcos de Niza, leader of the 1538 expedition, set off for Cíbola with a dozen Indians and Estevaníco as guide. Estevaníco carried the sacred copper rattle he had received from the Indians of southern New Mexico, and as he led the party over the desert, he met once again the devoted Children of the Sun. The poorest people, Father Marcos noted, possessed quantities of turquoise, which they said they received as payment for their labor in the Pueblo towns to the north. Four days from the sea, Father Marcos sent off a few Indians to find shells, pearls, and turquoises. Estevaníco continued on until he reached Whispering Spring, near Zuñi. Seeing the black man approach the sacred lake, whose waters shrouded the dwelling place of the dead, the Zuñi Bow Priests mistook Estevaníco first for an underworld kachina, then for a spy. They cut him to pieces.

Estevaníco's messenger staggered back to Marcos's camp, bearing a cross the size of a man. Estevaníco was dead. But within a thirty-day walk lay Cíbola, the richest country in the world.

Encouraged, Father Marcos trudged on until he reached the rise above the spring. Standing on the edge of the desert, the sun sinking into golden grains of sand, he beheld the adobe walls of the Zuñi town of Hawikuh transformed by golden light. Overcome by the long journey, the bloody death of the black slave, the pieces of turquoise in his hand, he remembered the Lord's trials in the wilderness, the twelve gates of Jerusalem, San Pedro's golden keys, Joshua's golden shield, the seven golden seals, King Solomon's golden treasure

Marcos planted two crosses, lifted his voice to the wind, and claimed the country for Spain. He fled back to Mexico City with the news. He had seen a city as big as Tenochtitlán with high walls made of shining stones and doors adorned with turquoises. He had found the Seven Cities of Gold!

As Don Francisco Vasquéz de Coronado, governor of Guadalajara, rode off from Compostela for the golden Seven Cities of Cíbola, his shadow turned the white walls an empty yellow. A hundred miles up the coast the earth itself turned yellow. The gilded trappings of the horses, shields, and bronze cannon caught in swirling dust. Golden cattle, sheep, and swine withered to the bone. Two hundred twenty-five gallants soaked and starved in their burnished armor. In sight of the Pacific sea, eleven hundred men were dying of thirst. They could not swat the flies. They could not ford the Yaqui River, so afraid were they of rust. At last, like the eight hundred Indian bearers straggling behind, they bared their skins to the sun. Their bodies were streaked in sweatlines that shone like gold seams. By the time the expedition crossed the Sierra Madre the men were transformed, "from the most brilliant company ever assembled in the Indies," into stinking goats and wretches.

Following the Pima and Opata guides across the Arizona desert, the explorers somehow missed the gold and silver mines near Tombstone. A small party sent off to explore the Grand Canyon peered down on the Colorado River, only eight feet wide from their mile-high vantage point, and decided the place was not worth mentioning.

At last the expedition reached the country of Cíbola and the Zuñi town of Hawikuh. "It is a little unattractive village, looking as if it had been crumpled all up together," wrote Pedro de Castañeda, chronicler of the expedition. "Such were the curses that some hurled at Friar Marcos that I pray God may protect him from them."

After four months on the trail, the desperate soldiers had some difficulty taking the village. The Zuñi pelted Coronado with stones and almost killed him. His weakened men nevertheless managed to continue their pillage, spitting the natives on lances, and looting the corn, which they now prized more than gold.

Coronado returned to Mexico City on a litter, having received a near-fatal horse kick in the head. He had spent a million dollars of his wife's money and lost half his men on the futile 1540 expedition. When he came before the tribunal and heard the charges of inept leadership laid against him, he could only mutter, "The land was sterile."

Heedless of Coronado's warnings, Don Juan de Oñate, in 1598, led 400 men, 130 families, 8 apostolic priests, and 7,000 head of cattle into the bare

Stark and elemental as nature, an early squash blossom necklace graces a Navajo elder. Photograph by Will Pennington.

New Mexican desert. Wagons carried church bells and gold smelters. Oñate made his fortune opening the gold and silver mines of Zacatecas and Sombrerete. Among the richest in Mexico, the mines also were the most dangerous, claiming the lives of thousands of "tamed" Chichimec laborers. The Indians Oñate encountered, potential slaves for the mines he would certainly discover, wore turquoise earrings, pendants, and collars. No one revealed any knowledge of gold or silver.

When the colonists reached El Paso on Holy Thursday, the friars, robed in thorns, sang prayers of thanks. Soldiers beat their backs with scourges. The earth ran red with blood. Then they walked the Road of the Dead Man over black rock, burning pebbles, and no water.

Two hundred miles north, on the banks of the Rio Grande, the settlers reached the Tewa town of Yunque. Oñate renamed it San Juan, built a church, and established the first Spanish colony. The Franciscan missionaries converted sixty thousand heathen souls. The conqueror exacted tribute payments of food and labor. For their refusal to submit, the people of Acoma endured a ruthless siege that lasted three days and nights. The survivors, by Oñate's order, had one foot chopped off; the chiefs were thrown off the precipice.

In a few years the settlers were starving. The new governor, Don Pedro de Peralta, moved the colony across the valley and named the new capital Santa Fé. Neither the conquistadors nor the friars had any idea where they were. They thought they had settled on a bleak peninsula south of China. Crimes against the natives went unpunished. Only the chronicler was brought to trial, for writing glowing accounts, beautiful but untrue.

The Seven Cities of Cíbola were not made of gold. But the Zuñi town of Hawikuh was a trade center prosperous enough to warrant tales of great wealth. Father Marcos de Niza noted that the town was as well known among the Pimas as is Mexico City in New Spain. The Indians of southern Arizona told the friar that the Zuñis used turquoise as money. The Indians of Sonora told explorer Melchior Díaz how Pueblo women wore their hair, twisted on each side and adorned with turquoises. Coronado encountered an Indian trader who said he had traveled from central Mexico to the land of the north. When the Antonio de Espejo expedition of 1582 arrived in Zuñi, they met Indians from Guadalajara.

Seven Zuñi towns sat at the crossroads of the turquoise trade. Zuñi merchants journeyed west to California, south along the Gila, Sonora, and Yaqui Rivers to the Pacific coast of Mexico, and east to the trading center of Pecos. From Pecos, turquoise, shells, and coral moved along the Kansas, Red, and

Pecos Rivers to Wichita, Kansas. Trade persisted between Zuñi and Sonora into the 1800s. In the mid-nineteenth century the Pueblos still made annual trading expeditions to the Pacific coast of Mexico, bartering buffalo robes, piñon nuts, and meat for conch shells and parrot plumes. Trade between the Pueblos and the Apaches and Teyas on the Plains had been active since 1300. Trading fairs were held regularly into the nineteenth century, commerce and dances even interrupting skirmishes and war.

The Southwestern rocks contained quartz, azurite, hematite, feldspar, opal, red ochre, jet, jasper, chalcedony, and malachite which the Indians used as healing stones, paint, and adornments. Coronado found garnets, peridot, and an abundance of turquoise near Pecos. Oñate discovered a blue silver, used as pigment, near Zuñi and malachite in Jemez. Captain Francisco Sanchez Chamuscado, in 1581, discovered the turquoise source in the Ortiz Mountains above Cerrillos. The entire northwest face of Mount Chalchihuitl had been cut away.

The Spaniards opened mines in the Sangre de Cristo Mountains near Taos and at Abo, near Albuquerque, extracting gold, silver, copper, and salt with Indian labor. The miners, climbing long notched poles, brought out the ore on their backs.

The old trade route through central Mexico became the Camino Real between Santa Fé and Mexico City. Wooden carts hauled supplies to the New Mexico missions. *Arrieros* drove long mule trains burdened with bullion, silver ore, tanned hides, and Indian blankets down through Zacatecas. Copper from the Santa Rita mines supplied Mexico City with twenty thousand mule-train loads a year. Gold and silver from the New World financed war against the Islamic Empire, against the Lutherans in Germany, and against the pirates on the high seas.

Cerrillos turquoise was shipped back to Spain. The finest stones became part of the Crown Jewels. Secreted away in the royal vaults of Toledo during World War II, they never have been found. Even

Aztec goldsmith making turquoise mosaic, Florentine codex

General Franco's ambitious search for the Crown Jewels proved futile. Crowns, rings, and mitres lie somewhere in the catacombs or have vanished, along with legendary Pre-Columbian mosaics adorned with Cerrillos turquoises.

I left Mexico one day
on the road to Santa Fé
and on the road I read
an inscription on a coin that said:
I left Mexico one day
on the road to Santa Fé

—*Cuentos de nunca acabar*

In the streets of Mexico City the merchants outrang the clang of the conquistadors. Mexican fops and their painted ladies strutted in silks and lace from France, wool from Flanders, and gems from the East, drank rum from Jamaica and wines from Spain out of Venetian goblets, dined off Chinese porcelain, rode in carriages drawn by Arabian stallions, and wrote love notes on Italian paper.

The Spaniards gave to the New World the horse, which had ranged across America ten thousand years before and had become extinct before it had grown to full size. They brought to Southwestern architecture the corner chimney, which they had borrowed from the Moors.

The serpent of the Garden of Eden proved more cunning than Quetzalcoatl. The Cross supplanted the corn stalk. The sacrifice of Our Lord on the Tree ended the blood sacrifice of thousands to the god of the sun. Among the Indian population Christ became synonymous with the sun and the Virgin with the moon. The Greek physician and deity Aesculapius became Saint Esquipoulas, whose shrines welcome pilgrims from Guatemala to New Mexico.

The Spaniards named the chalchihuitl "jade" because they believed the stone was efficacious in curing diseases of the liver. Turquoise decorated bridles, because the stone would protect horses from stumbling and riders from falling off their horses.

Indian coppersmiths had forged the iron weapons of the conquerors. From the fittings stripped from Cortés's ships they made steel swords that felled the Aztecs in battle. After the Conquest, Indian smiths were forbidden to work or own metals. Skilled craftsmen emigrated from Europe and metallurgists from China. By the seventeenth century, Indians were permitted to serve as apprentices. Once they mastered European methods, they were embellishing cathedral altars with angels, flowers, scallop shells, and dolphins in gold, silver, lapis, and turquoise. Jewelers fashioned crosses for the friars, *milagros* for the saints, filigreed butterflies for the necks of Spanish ladies, and bands of yellow gold, red gold, and "wedded metals." Smiths made stirrups and horseshoes of silver. They outfitted Spanish overlords with silver spurs and Charro costumes studded with silver buttons. The Devil, it was said, dressed as a charro as he rode his black stallion through the night.

In 1560, Vasco de Quiroga, bishop of Michoacán, established Christian communities on Lake Pàtzcuaro, in the shadow of the ruins of Tzintzuntzan. In that "happy place" the Tarascans were to practise a primitive communism inspired by Sir Thomas More's Utopia, the ideal state the English cleric had envisioned in the New World. Believing that the Indians were innocent sons of Adam and Eve rather than beasts in human form, Quiroga set up schools to reteach the Tarascans the arts they had been forced to abandon by the conquistadors. Half a cen-

A young Navajo, Tom Toslino, photographed upon his arrival at Carlisle School, Pennsylvania, the boarding institution established to retrain and acculturate Native American boys and girls. His Pueblo-style necklace substitutes silver crosses for silver squash blossoms. Photograph by John N. Choate, c. 1880.

Painted in serpents and crosses, Mescalero Apache dancers revive the mountain spirits. Photographer unknown, c. 1950.

tury before, Princess Erendira led the Tarascan forces against the Spaniards. Following their brutal defeat, the Indians threw their gold ornaments into the lake. Now the Tarascans worked as slaves in the gold, silver, and copper mines of Michoacàn while the Indians living on the lake hammered out copper plates, bowls, and jugs for the kitchens of the Spanish lords.

Some say a mining disaster following a century of hard labor in the turquoise mines of Cerrillos precipitated the Pueblo Revolt of 1680. Others say it was the epidemic and drought, when Indians and colonists were reduced to eating boiled hides. The Spaniards blamed the Indians and their infernal religion for years of unrelieved hardships. Despite repeated castigations, the Pueblos continued to offer feathers and turquoises to their idols. Forty-seven Pueblo shamans were tried for sorcery and hanged. Popé, a medicine man from San Juan Pueblo, planned the massive uprising.

On the Sunday of Wrath, twenty-four towns rose as one against their oppressors. Pueblo warriors murdered five hundred Spaniards, twenty-one friars, and kidnapped the women. They destroyed the churches. They burned the wheat. Baptized Indians jumped into the river and rubbed their skins with amole plants to cleanse themselves of the Vatican oils.

Armed with arquebus and sword, the chiefs rode to the walls of the Palace of the Governors in Santa Fé and presented two crosses, the red cross for resistance, the white for surrender. After three days without food and water, the Spaniards raised the white cross. Then they filed out, retreating south to Mexico. Indians from Isleta and Piro joined the retreat. The rebels moved into the Palace and turned it into a pueblo. They celebrated the flight of their foreign masters, the redemption of their parched lands.

News of the rebellion spurred revolts among the Janos and Sumas living near Casas Grandes. The Apaches, who had been sent to work in the mines of Chihuahua twenty years before, went on a wild rampage through northern Mexico.

Don Diego de Vargas, Zapata y Lujan Ponce de Leon, rode into New Mexico twelve years later in search of quicksilver. Having distinguished himself as the justice of a mining camp and protector of the royal supply of quicksilver, he was granted the governorship of the desert. Quicksilver was essential in processing gold and silver ores. Used by Indians as cinnabar pigment, the quicksilver to be found in the vicinity of Hopi was reportedly so fine it lay in pools of liquid mercury.

At first de Vargas tried friendly persuasion. He offered to end forced labor and to pardon the rebels,

An Apache boy, rounded up with thousands of Navajo captives on the Long Walk to Bosque Redondo, near Ft. Sumner, New Mexico. There they were held without adequate food, shelter, or clothing between 1864 and 1868. Survivors were granted a permanent reservation, the region the Navajos occupy today.

if they agreed to submit to Spanish rule. Pueblos fled to the mountains or joined nomadic tribes on the Great Plains. After executing seventy warriors and enslaving four hundred defenders of the Palace of the Governors, de Vargas pacified his province. He never found a trace of mercury.

Eventually the Spaniards resettled the land. With the help of Indian labor, the friars built adobe missions. The huge bronze bell at Acoma was acquired in Zacatecas, in exchange for twelve Apache children. Isolated in small mountain towns and open valleys, Spanish settlers frequently banded together with the Pueblos in defense against raiding Apaches. Interdependence led to similarities in architecture and an interweaving of folklore strains. Old and New World demons traded plots.

The Spaniards renamed the surviving pueblos along the Rio Grande for Spanish saints. They renamed the rivers and mountains. The Indians assumed Spanish names. The Hopis began raising sheep. The Navajos adopted horses, which they rode on raids against Pueblo and Spanish settlements. The Pueblos accepted those saints that protected realms the kachinas had not foreseen.

When the Navajos descended upon the western mesas they adopted Hopi customs and crafts. In time, they borrowed weaving designs from Saltillo blankets, brought by Mexican merchants, and learned silverworking techniques from itinerant craftsmen from Mexico.

The stars, planets, and constellations spinning over the New World bear the names of the gods of ancient Greece.

The discovery of placer gold at Sierra del Oro in the Ortiz Mountains, in 1828, started the first gold rush west of the Mississippi. As soon as the news reached Missouri, prospectors and gold panners were following mountain men and traders out on the Santa Fé Trail and into the mountains. At the height of the Cerrillos Boom, in 1879, miners were finding silver, lead, and zinc and had opened 130 mines. At Golden, great chunks of gold ran through the native quartz. There was gold in the Sangre de Cristo and gold in the Sandia Mountains. Placer gold at Elizabethtown started a stampede. The Bridle Chamber at Lake Valley produced one of the richest silver bonanzas in the world.

Further south, in the Organ Mountains, fifty silver mines were operating by 1867. Then came the huge finds at Silver City. Near the prehistoric turquoise workings at Hachita, prospectors found so much silver they called the region "Eureka."

Decloizite, vanadinite, and red crystals of vandamite lay in the region of Octaroon. Mountains shone with garnets, azurite, and gold. "The wealth of the world," wrote Alexander von Humboldt, "will

Spectators arrive in buckboards to observe the feast day of San Geronimo at Taos Pueblo. During this popular celebration, *Koshare* clowns shinny up a high pole, a brave burlesque that ends with the rescue of a dead sheep. Later, the clowns shower the crowd with candies and gifts. Photograph by Z. P. Stewart, c. 1900.

Photographed at their campsite, Navajo women display abundant turquoise strands and unadorned *concha* belts worn at the turn of the century. Photograph by Ben Wittick.

be found in New Mexico and Arizona." Prospectors were earning up to a hundred dollars a day. By the end of the century the prehistoric turquoise mines at Hachita and Orogrande were being worked again. Mount Chalchihuitl was yielding $1 million worth of turquoise a year.

There were troubles, of course. Ulysses S. Grant, president of the San Pedro and Canon de l'Agua Co. in the New Placers District of the Sandia Mountains, remarked on the scarcity of water. Miners faced so many Apache attacks that four forts were built to protect their interests. For years there had been a bounty on Apache scalps. By 1863, troops were patrolling the Sandia Mountains, ordered to kill every Navajo and Apache in sight. The infantry under Brigadier General James E. Carleton destroyed crops, herds, and hogans and rounded up thousands of Navajos on a four-hundred-mile march to Bosque Redondo, where they remained in captivity, naked and starving, throughout the Civil War.

Now most of the gold is played out. The gold bells that rang across the mountain valleys are as silent as the Cities That Died of Fear. The road between the ghost town of Golden and Cedar Crest is called the Turquoise Trail.

Tales entice unwary prospectors to the Superstition Mountains. A vein of horn silver, hidden by Indians, lies somewhere in the Sandia Mountains.

Legend has it that Montezuma sent his treasure of gold to Arizona and the Papagos buried the gold under Casa Grande. Someday his spirit will bequeath his wealth to the Indians.

Near Tucson, a mountain of noises is home to thousands of singing birds that nest in walls of silver. A three-tongued devil guards the mother lode of the Silver Night Mine. A cobra defends the entrance of a mine near Mogollon. A blue flame protects the tunnel of a secret mine in the Gila Wilderness. The army protects the gold deposits hidden in a cave near Orogrande. Strange vapors rise from the "X" scratched on a treasure map hidden in the shank of an old man's knife. In the mountains above El Paso, the setting sun at winter solstice strikes a perpendicular rock. There lies the treasure.

Northern Traditional Dancer dressed in hawk feathers. Gallup Intertribal Ceremonial.

Teepees at Red
Rock State Park,
Arizona, lived
in by Pueblo con-
testants at the
Gallup Intertribal
Ceremonial.

Rainbow colors of Pendleton blankets have been popular since Yankee peddlers introduced them in the nineteenth century. Sisters Olympia Pena and Gregorita Baca observe a Buffalo Dance on Christmas Day, San Ildefonso Pueblo.

The symbol of the world directions radiates on a Hopi rattle. Shaken seeds play the sound of rain. The course of the sun is the round course of the seasons and the source of the colors of the world. The Zuñi dancer wears a Zuñi bracelet and Navajo *concha* belt and *ketoh*.

Little Zuñi dancer dresses like a grown-up in an oversized squash blossom necklace. Young and old participate in the dances, which celebrate the Father and Mother Creators and the generations of the four worlds. Gallup Intertribal Ceremonial.

Ann Coho, a Ramah Navajo, beads ornaments, time-consuming work that few women practice. Glass beads were introduced by Spaniards and, later, traders from the east. Many designs seen today were derived from Plains and Woodland tribes as well as the Huicholes of Mexico. The Coho family lives near Ramah, on the border of the Zuñi reservation.

Navajo woman binds her daughter's hair in traditional style. Calico skirts and blouses, patterned after nineteenth-century pioneer dress, are standard costume for daily and ceremonial wear.

Educator, activist, and spiritual guide, Ben Barney is a traditional Navajo, who traces his lineage back ten generations. As former director of the Navajo Community College in Window Rock, he worked tirelessly to install native language and literature courses in school curricula. When he's not roaming the highlands of Chiapas and Guatemala, he lives as a shepherd on his ancestral lands in the Chuska Mountains of Arizona.

Beauty before me,
With it I wander.
Beauty behind me,
With it I wander.
Beauty below me,
With it I wander.
Beauty above me,
With it I wander.
Beauty all around
 me,
With it I wander.
In old age traveling,
With it I wander.
On the beautiful trail
 I am,
With it I wander.
     —from Navajo
         Night Chant

Shirley Abrahamson,
professional dancer,
Colville Reservation,
Washington State.

Chester Mahooty leads a professional troupe of dancers and drummers throughout the United States and Europe. He is a world traveler whose roots are in the red rocks of Zuñi. His spectacular turquoise ornaments are his own creation. Photographed at Church Rock, Arizona.

As part of her coming-of age ceremony, the young Navajo woman Tanya Garne Nez sprinkles sacred corn pollen on corn batter that was just poured over corn husks lining the round cooking pit. The huge pancake will bake overnight and be served the following day, during the feast celebrating her twelfth birthday.

Corn is the staff of life, and the grinding of corn is an essential ceremony. The stone rolling pin and stone slab, *mano* and *metate*, are household tools almost as old as corn. Yellow corn represents sunlight; white corn, clouds and ice; red corn, blood; and blue corn, summer.

A Navajo woman
visits her child-
hood home in
Canyon de Chelly.
Her ancestors
occupied the
canyon for cen-
turies before they
were driven out
by army troops
under Kit Carson
in 1864. The Nava-
jos returned in
1868, and today
families spend the
summers grazing
sheep, tending
fields, and raising
fruit trees in the
shadow of cliff
dwellings built by
the "Ancient Ones,"
the Anasazis.

Maud Chee Yazzie, a Navajo living near Vanderwagen, New Mexico, and her dog.

The Pueblo woman keeps time for the dancers, the singers, for her children's children, and those who have come before. Land, home, and property belong to her and descend through her, as the center of a traditional matriarchal society. Here, Blue Corn marks time on a drum made of cottonwood and deerskin.

You are a precious stone, a turquoise. You have been formed, shaped, you have the color; you are the off-shoot and the stem.
—Aztec, words for children

Tom Mauchahty
Ware, a Kiowa/
Comanche,
chanting at the
Gallup Intertribal
Ceremonial.

Kachinas are ancestral spirits, intermediaries between the gods and the people. The kachinas live in the mountains and under the lakes and visit the Hopis and Zuñis for the six-month cycle of ceremonies following the winter solstice.

Home is the wall
of clay and straw,
a village of rooms
reached by lad-
ders, divided by
winter and sum-
mer and a clear
river running
through. Woman
of Taos Pueblo,
photographed in
1971.

Where no roads go, the mountains are hard company. In summer the rain walks, and in winter snow drifts so high there is no way out, on two legs or four.

A Hopi man, leaning against his house wall, sews in the sun. The village of Old Oraibi is the longest continuously inhabited settlement on the continent—the center of the world.

Turquoise Boy carries the sun, and when he rides his turquoise horse the cloudless skies are the color of turquoise. Ann Coho and baby, safe in his cradle board.

Percy Romero of Cochiti Pueblo prepares a package of gifts for a friend who stopped by on All Saints' Day. Hospitality, sharing food, even with strangers, are time-honored customs. Much comes from little. Gifts are inexhaustible.

Louise Cly prepares a barbeque in her backyard, Monument Valley.

Cordi Gomez pulls
hot loaves from
the *horno*, the
adobe oven in
back of her home
in Pojoaque Pueblo.

Guests line up for the wedding feast of Karen Little and Richard Toledo in Crystal, New Mexico.

Ben Barney prepares a meal in the lean-to on his summer grazing lands in the Chuska Mountains, Arizona.

Relatives of the bride and groom, seated at the rear of the hogan, celebrate with a wedding feast of Navajo specialties. The couple was married by a Christian minister and then by a Navajo shaman. Soon the elders will fill their ears with good advice on how to have a happy marriage.

Every day Pueblo and Navajo jewelers display their work under the portal of the Palace of the Governors, located on the main plaza in Santa Fé. Turquoise, hishi, *concha* belts, ear cuffs, bangles, fetishes, nuggets, beads, collectibles, affordables, to suit every budget and made by hand.

Verna Williamson, former governor of Isleta Pueblo, was the first woman elected to office among the Pueblos.

Nathaniel Chee, Sr., a Mescalero Apache shaman, blesses a handful of turquoise beads while holding a pouch filled with sacred yellow corn pollen and pieces of turquoise. The Mescalero Apaches, who live in the forested mountains of southern New Mexico, cling to a vanishing language and culture. It always rains at the end of the rain dance in Mescalero.

Turquoise wards off bad spells and evil wishes, says Nathaniel Chee, Sr. Power lies in stones that speak of time, space, and vast belief whirling in the hand.

The Pueblos journeyed from the underworld waters, the Navajos came from the stars. Home is the middle place, the center, "finished in beauty." Billy Wahnee, Sr., is a Comanche living in Tuba City, Arizona, at the edge of the Hopi reservation.

CHAPTER 5

COYOTE'S SEARCH

FOR THE

LAKE OF JEWELS

VILLA VICIOSA

San Cristóbal de las Casas sits like a bishop in a deep chair, a church on both armrests, a mountain at his back. His eye upon the raining sky, he is praying for civility, an orange, less weather. In front of the cathedral a pack of dogs snaps at scraps of fat.

Bells are counting out the steps of morning waders. Maya Indians pour through the streets as if they were born carrying sacks of charcoal that turn them black, wooden chairs stacked like ladders on their backs, straw hats stacked on their heads, baskets brimming with oyster mushrooms, shitakes, and yuyus, bundles of calla lilies, bromeliads, and tree orchids.

Tzotzil and Tzeltal Maya come down to the market to sell and buy corn, pigs, salt, beans, candles, rockets, tin funnels, plastic sandals, rope, wrenches, clay pots, used pants, medicine, fruit, a goat, a Coke. The women are always running, balancing babies and nets of dried fish. The men get haircuts, spread news, get drunk, go home in the dark carrying orange crates, carnations, a child's coffin, white.

The Indians and Ladinos meet on the streets of the city, trade but seldom mingle, divided by culture and money and by deep wounds inflicted by history and human failing. They call each other dogs, and the saints and gods in the churches and mountains for miles around hear it.

"One of the meanest cities in all America," wrote Father Thomas Gage, an English friar who traveled through the Chiapas highlands of southern Mexico in the seventeenth century. The merchants "are close-handed and the gentlemen hard and sparing, wanting of wit and courtiers' parts and bravery." The men make a meal of beans, pick their teeth, and think it's a banquet. The women are capable of poisoning a priest. San Cristóbal, judged the friar, "is no fit place for Jesuits."

The Ladinos get rich selling the souls of Indians to the devil. The Earth Lord, say the Indians, is a fat Ladino who owns all the land, all the water, and all the earth's treasures.

Nothing was invented here but a heavy sandal, thick as nerves. Before the Spanish Conquest, the Maya of Zinacantán dominated the highlands, controlling the trade in salt. Today Zinacantecs raise chrysanthemums in greenhouses that float like caterpillar tents on the naked mountainsides. Zinacantec truckers transport cut flowers as far away as Mexico City. By the side of the road Zinacantec boys sell "God's eyes" made of bright yarn, a design they borrowed from the Huichol Indians of northwestern Mexico. The Maya of Chamula, who held off Cortés's siege by throwing golden diadems down from the citadels to Bernal Díaz and his soldiers, still have a reputation for rebelliousness. Most Chamula men work as day laborers, as migrant workers in California, or as waiters in resort towns like Cancún. Chamula women raise sheep and weave woolen garments for the Maya of the highlands. In the busy tourist spots Chamula women and children sell woven bracelets and belts and bright bags bought from Guatemalan traders. Tzeltal vendors hawk earrings and beads of amber from the ancient mines in Simojovel. The men of Chalchihuitan sell fool's gold wrapped in deer hide and hooves. Maya villagers of Chalchihuitan have never found jade or turquoise caches and have no idea how their town got the name of Green or Blue Stone.

Occasionally the Lacandones journey to San Cristóbal to sell bows and arrows. The quetzal feathers, coveted by Maya and Aztec lords, have all but vanished with the jungle. In exchange for a rainforest of mahogany the Lacandones own Swatches and tape recorders.

The Indians go home to villages rooted in earth and rock. Imported hardware shaves the fields. Power marches in line up the hills like wired crucifixes. The television tower flashes its magic red pulse to no one all night. Below the telephone poles witches plant their seeds in irresistible rows. Government helicopters drop insurance policies from the clouds, trombones play in mountain caves. Saint Christopher walks barefoot through the puddles. The conqueror's bronze horse topples in rising water.

The presence of something other walks beside the road, beside the foot path winding up the slopes; on the vertical corn fields and cliffs the mist is lifting ridge after ridge. Something flutters in the rocks, hovers in the shape of hills changing with the light. Shadows fall on the blue crosses standing at every waterhole, cave entrance, and grave: blue intersections between heaven, earth, and the underworld.

Life is hard, change an illusion, progress a bitter need and a mortal corruption. Actors in a mystery play of miracles and suffering, people live on the edge of truth and nothingness. Tragedy stops the passage of time. Poverty masquerades as a dark blessing, the unknowable as grace, moving through prayers and noise, alarming gold, mud, and dust, black thatch, rags, and bandage, worn walls without a message.

The lords watch and listen and with inexplicable reason summon yet another calamity. The Maya offer candles, bargain, beg, confine saints to a dark and cobwebbed corner, withholding praise for withheld health and blessings. They stage extravagant fiestas celebrating their happiness and good fortune.

Once a saint came to town in a wooden cart drawn by two mules. The cart rang with pots and pans and all sorts of amulets and charms. He set up his camp by the lake and people started coming. The Indians offered him corn and coins and he cured their sicknesses. He had a long white beard and people called him Grandfather. "I make people feel better," he said. He said he was a knife sharpener from Cuicuila, but everyone knew he was a saint.

The Ladino pharmacists didn't like him and tried to drive him out. The Zoques offered him land. The Zinacantecs offered him a house and musicians who would play for him twenty-four hours a day. He left without a word, driving his cart down the mountain road to the Pacific coast.

CITY OF MIRRORS

Oaxaca is one of those rare cities dedicated to infinite repetition. Under the enormous trees of the plaza a brass band plays as people circle in the Sunday *paseo.* Bassoons and giraffe balloons keep time to the music. Gardenias float in the pond. Round and round little girls are skipping or hiding in the shrubs. Round and round the vendors go, parading rugs in Navajo designs. Necklaces of agate and amethyst swing from their arms.

On the baroque facade of Santo Domingo Cathedral brown apostles are talking in their sleep. Saint Dominic slumps in the center, posing as a Preconquest king. His robed feet rest on a round medallion elaborate as a bird's nest. Out of the nest dives a stone dove, which hovers above the heads of Christ and a saint, who are holding a model of the house of God. The ceiling of the cathedral is dense with cherubim tangled in golden foliage. Inside the monastery a Mixtec diving bird made of gold carries a gold butterfly in its beak.

In the market thousands of clay churches sit one atop the other, bells silent, tower upon tower. On hill after hill in the surrounding valley the true churches rise, mosaic domes sparkling in sunlit yellow or blue. Huge nesting birds perched on golden mounds, they are calling the Olmec chieftains, Zapotec lords and ladies drowsing in the ruins below, singing of the house of God set to reign above defeated cities, domes and towers sinking, too, into ruin, church windows cracked and dark, roofs open to the sky and cries of real crows.

Byzantine domes in a Byzantine desert, transplanted to a land where the greatest craftsmen worked for Mixtec, Toltec, and Aztec nobles, casting golden gods, frogs, and singing birds. Time was a turquoise-blue mosaic circle, a bevelled mirror set in serpent-etched tumbaga. The modern smiths of Oaxaca replicate the animals and birds of ancient Monte Albán so faithfully it is as if it is their sacred duty to reforge life and history. They hammer Maltese crosses and Moorish moons. Masters of mosaic, lost-wax, granulation, and repoussé, their ancestors achieved a style that is Byzantine in detail, and in a Byzantine irony, matched the skills of smiths working at the same time in the guild shops of Constantinople.

Santa Sophia grants the divine kings rest where they lie under the necropoli of Monte Albán and Mitla. Folk go on living with protective talismans around their necks and the scent of gardenias. The god of spring is imminent. The god of fire is every old man hunched over his son as he pounds gold sheet. Smiths made the turquoise gems, the green cliffs, the stones of the city, the blue-eyed birds, the golden butterfly, the angels, the saints, the leaves of the trees, the souls selling stones in the park.

way through dense foliage. When they stepped into the sacred precinct, they witnessed the jaguar guardians whole, the serpent mask complete, and the legendary jewels fixed in their sockets. As young lovers they had seen the clear turquoise eyes of the eagles, the burning emerald eyes of the jaguar. Now they leaned on their canes. Quetzalcoatl, they reminded me, enjoyed only one night of passion and in penance drove the world into darkness. Then he buried his treasures in the mountains and went away.

QUERETERO

Young men come from the trees to the plaza, white shirt pockets blushing with cherry opals, pants pockets heavy with Mexican opals, red fires flaming inside. In their palms they hold fire agates, rainbows arcing across a burnt ochre sky.

THE CHICAMEC SEA

Along the tracks, geraniums growing in cans hang from motionless trains. At dawn women sweep out the cars. Girls scrub clothes on the gangplanks to the freight doors and tie them up to choke. By afternoon children flee from green desks in green boxcars. They run as fast as they can but cannot outrun the schoolhouse moving on the horizon.

At dusk other women bring in the wash and light the lamps others farther on will snuff out. Men who rode off that morning are still riding and will never reach home. The lamps blinking in tumbled rooms turn to stars. Across the wasteland of the Chichimec Sea sleepwalkers roam free.

The Chicasaw woman from Minnesota is making her first trip to Mexico. She's married to a man from a little mining town north of Zacatecas. "Nothing's the same," she says. "My people wear beaded roses. Our clothes, our customs, our songs are completely different. We don't even eat the same food. We've been married for twenty-two years. He's afraid of the woods. We have nothing in common."

MALINALCO

Once the wind god spoke, the warriors left Tenochtitlán for the wild canyons of Malinalco. In the wind they heard the roar of jaguars and the sound of eagles. In wind caves they saw portraits of their animal souls. As they climbed, their limbs acquired wings and claws. The cliff possessed the scarred eyes of the serpent, its mouth the yawning wind. Cutting deeper, the warriors released the shapes within. Here their hearts would ascend to heaven.

Weathered jaguars guard the temple steps. A serpent's forked tongue forms the threshold. In its open jaws glow a stone eagle bowl, a pair of eagles, and a solitary jaguar. The round sacrificial altar faces south, the eagle ready to take flight when the wind blows across the chasm. The wind is visible in the rockscape, which has been carved by currents ever since Quetzalcoatl set this world in motion with his breath. The wind has its source, townsfolk say, in the channel of caves beneath the sacred shrine of Chalma; it rushes under the mountains, up the fissures, and escapes through the eagle's beak, a whisper, then a long hiss. The Aztecs, after centuries of wandering, heard one exhalation and returned to their beginnings in the cliffs to sculpt this final, kiva-like temple in the rock.

Malinalco is famous among sorcerers, an elderly couple told me as we climbed the trail to the summit. They were making their last pilgrimage. Years before, they had to scale boulders and hack their

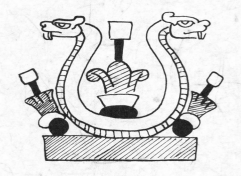
Moon with serpent, Mixtec codex

ZACATECAS

Zacatecas is a city of extravagant artifice. The pink stones have turned themselves into banks, post offices, launderettes, and long cafés where businessmen speculate on the durability of gold-leafed vines and angel wings. Students sip sodas in the anterooms of Spanish counts. In the candy stalls, once royal storage rooms, silver bars of chocolate mount to the rafters. Marble lovers embrace in the glorious parks. In the Garden of Mothers little girls play politely in long white dresses. In the plaza by the market a bronze musician plucks at his bronze harp, his patriotic hymn ringing out for bins of sweet buns and vegetables, armies of pigeons, and Huichol women selling popcorn on the curbs. Saints prefer the substantial hush of the cathedrals, where their every wish is indulged. Once the Virgin asked for a gold ring and the Franciscan brothers, though vowed to poverty, complied. Monasteries are temples of art, exhibiting Indian bronzes, Tibetan tonkas, and Picasso etchings but not the Pre-Columbian art of the region. Mexican baroque stuns history into disbelief. The empty arches of the aqueduct form a more perfect monument. It is hard to find Zacatecas.

Above the stone city rises a random purple, green, and white city. Perpendicular streets coil so steeply it is futile to drive and maddening to walk. Zacatecans complain of the hills underlying their city, the impossibility of living here or exiting. Cob-

bles sink into blind ravines, twisted alleys lead to a maze of houses teetering on outcrops, rooms leaning outside in. Shoes in the shoemaker's shop are always slipping and walking off, watches in the repair shop eternally tilt toward five o'clock, stones in the stone cutter's shop avalanche in rude piles of amethyst, hematite, and turquoise, the shops themselves stranded, the tailor's clothes swaying on metal hangers fit for lopsided people with uneven arms and legs. The inhabitants of Zacatecas possess extraordinary chiseled features and are unusually long of limb. Daily they must circle and climb tirelessly to reach a neighbor, friend, or loved one and usually surrender prematurely under the strain. This is why lovers and married couples are mismatched.

Under the hills run the deepest and most treacherous mine shafts in the New World. The silver that built the cathedral and supported half of Europe came out of the mine called Eden. Infamous cruelty revenges itself in the bones of the people.

Now even the most prosperous live like miners above the perilous shafts, making tunnels of their cavernous churches, tunnels of their narrow houses, tunnels of their streets, always groping, toiling upward.

the blasted mines every night. They whistle because everything in life has been pried open, and the treasures—a peso, a clean shirt, a secret of the heart—shine on the common surface.

CHALCHIHUITES

If you go to Chalchihuites you will ride for miles through green and yellow valleys, see an occasional hacienda, an occasional cowboy loping west across the range, and when the hills turn red and range grass gives way to swollen rock, you will know you are coming to the country of mines. The sun will turn away, and you will remember the town of Chalchihuites and its red octagonal plaza always in shade and know the dark side of the frontier, four empires, layer upon layer, fallen and still not free. The stone road struggling past earthen walls will narrow. A plain half village scattered on the flats will finally disappear. You must cross the black river, dogs and naked children splashing in the cascades, and beyond fields of red weeds, you will arrive, as a pilgrim to the rock, in the ruined city of Alta Vista, crossroads of the New World, crown of the turquoise culture, directly on the Tropic of Cancer.

The burnt columns of the palace are in alignment with the cosmos. Shadows on the landscape move like a clock. Toward the west, a mesa drops into blackness. Toward the east, the sun strikes a perfect glowing peak made of malachite. Chalchihuites Mountain marks the summer solstice.

One thousand miles north, on the edge of Santa Fé, stands its blue brother, Mt. Chalchihuitl. Linked by name and by ancient trails, the mountains remain companions in a great geological chain. In subterranean strata, crystalline floes are forming and hardening with the seasons and shifting poles. Tides of rain create the only measurable difference between them. The sun, too, must create a subtle chemistry as it returns to settle on this ground, altering waters, changing turquoise to drier green.

SOMBRERETE

One can imagine anything happening here, a riderless white horse wild in the street, a lunatic showering silver coins on the plaza, a sudden explosion of light that turns the town back to stone. The people of Sombrerete are characters in a Spanish chronicle where, along with the names of past and future inhabitants, run the blotched accounts of gains and losses, the yearly tonnage of silver, the fates of nations, kings, Juans, and Marias. No one troubles over price. Marias stroll the streets in threes or lean in yellow doorways dreaming of princes. Around the fountain old women dream they are waltzing in black gowns. Old men under enormous sombreros dream of the sky as they steady the white pillars of the portico or shuffle in their odd square sandals down the road. They are dreaming themselves awake. They are dreaming themselves asleep and dreaming. Their eyes, blood, and hair are clotted with silver. The air echoes with laughter.

No one smiles. No one speaks. Men whistle. They emit canary tones when they have seen a beautiful woman or have won a bet. The notes are the same because every day the same beautiful woman gives the same lusty signal. The bet has been won so many times, the prize passed back and forth through calloused hands has taken on the sheen of burnished metal. Where men own nothing they trade their luck. They whistle because they shovel

BATOPILAS

The town called Near the River meets the river and the bottom of the canyon at the same time and place. The church is whiter than foam. White houses polished as boulders are brighter than silver dusting the river. The air is hotter than a mine. Guarding the narrow gorge are the red walls of a medieval castle built by Alexander Shepherd, last governor of Washington, D.C. Under brick turrets young couples live in rooms like rafts washed up in mud yards loud with ranchero music, pigs, and roosters. If men pan enough silver or acquire enough quills of gold dust, their households may float to one of the abandoned houses in midtown, whose roofless walls temporarily serve as stalls for black cattle.

The end of Batopilas is the domain of the old, who spend the day prospecting for gossip under the clock tower and the evening cheering soccer on a black and white set crackling on a bench in the plaza. The grand mansions of the silver barons date from a period unknown in the world above the Copper Canyon. Spontaneous Greek columns, Spanish grilles, Gothic arches, and Moorish domes capture the eccentric air of a seaside resort. Green doors stay shut. Wooden doors wear bolts. Peeling doors belong to shopkeepers who make profits on oranges and rare avocados. Red doors lead to empty parlors lined with velvet chairs and long corridors reaching back to the river.

The most peculiar rift runs down the middle of the single meandering street. People facing east are pleasant, energetic, and blunt, people facing west, reckless and suspicious. Two centuries ago, Don Rafael Alonzo de Pastraño paved the path from his house to the church in pure silver ingots for the visit of the Bishop of Durango, who participated in the wedding procession of the don's daughter after damning his host for his ostentatious display of wealth. Now the cobbles are dusty copper. The current priest is unable to cross the road. He stands on the sullen side, fearful, even on his birthday, of the truck without a clutch, of two riders on horseback wearing shoulder rifles. A battle rages between the priest and the doctor, the owner of the hardware store and the man whose claim, he says, is unrecorded. Doña Noncé warns me to keep my business secret. Everyone asks what I know.

Forty-million-year-old volcanic uplifts made the canyon. Fractured, densely veined, and under tons of granite, the deepest ore deposits are at eye level. The Spanish *adelantados*, following a wind of rumors, picked their way from the Pacific coast into this skeletal landscape. Exhausted, they stopped to bathe on the narrow bank below the suspension bridge. Silver coated their bodies and their hair. They stood in the shallows, shining in native silver, purer than the silver of Taxco, Pachuca, Zacatecas, or Guanajuato. They had discovered the largest silver anomaly in the world. Silver grows in herringbone patterns, in wire coils, and in leaves. The rarest specimens are ruby red. Since 1632, 3 billion ounces have been extracted by miners and slave labor from three hundred mines named for saints, ghosts, the divine shepherd, swallows, horses, and George Washington.

Surrounded by a mineral halo, the people of Batopilas are crystalline or metallic, steely as a trigger or happy as leaves. Every one of them is searching for richer veins. Silver dust poisons their blood, makes them lie like thieves, or plates their eyes in revery.

The Tarahumara Indians, whose ancestors slaved in the mines, live in caves high in the canyons. They are personifications of fractures, their faces split. When they come to town they sit motionless under lime trees or against a wall, watching schoolgirls in satin dresses, the plump nuns who teach at the school of Sor Juana Inez de la Cruz, and the cowboys and gunmen mingling in front of city hall. They are shadows, who will sweep the floor, water the dry papayas, sprint through the heat from one end of town to the other on an errand, or hoist beams as big as crosses in return for a few pesos or a cigarette. They align themselves with the cliffs. They dance on the ledges, dressed in flowers and butterfly cocoons. They eat peyote, watch the rock change into colors, and wait for portents. This life is a steppingstone to another reality.

they will be first with the triumphant news
the day we leap the wall
of the five senses.

—*Alfonso Reyes*
from Tarahumara Herbs

The mother lode is in their keeping and they are dying out with the secret.

CASAS GRANDES

Many travelers have come before. The city, even in ruins, is a good place to sleep. Clouds drowse on mountain crests. Yellow wildflowers, the size of coins, grow as calm as the sun in its simple movement across the sand. The round temple platforms welcome breezes. Light opens room after room. There are many pebbled courts in which to lie. Walls advancing into earth are a comfort.

All who pause at this station—traders, conquerors, Apache raiders—hitch their horses and move on. Cabeza de Vaca, Coronado, and General Ibarra crossed the valley when the tide was flat as glass. Explorers Adolph Bandelier and Carl Lumholz marveled at the huge mud walls, destroyed and thus preserved by fire. Left alone, the city waits on the angular borders between wakefulness and dreams.

Irrigated water flows through the valley once more. Mennonites drive their wagons to green farms in the distance. It is eternal spring. Apple orchards mile after mile and turquoise the color of a robin's egg.

THE CITY OF HOLY FAITH OF SAINT FRANCIS OF ASSISI

The Santa Fé River falls from the snowline through aspen forests, juniper canyons, and banks of cottonwoods, a natural trail between mountains and desert. Water runs on and off with the seasons through the heart of Santa Fé before wandering out to die under distant buttes. The river is the reason for the city.

An older pueblo lies underneath the center of Santa Fé, under the Palace of the Governors, banks, hotels, and offices, the haberdashers and the Gospel Café, under the pueblo-style indoor parking garage, the Norman-inspired cathedral, and shops selling Indian jewelry and blankets along the Old Santa Fé Trail. When foreign investors decide to dig a new foundation or when something goes wrong with the water and telephone lines, repairmen and construction workers must enter this older town, whose roofs are a mesh of wires and pipes. Its existence is sporadic, like the river, dependent on the whims of nature and human folly.

When the Spaniards came, the Indians moved across the river. Houses that were part of the Indian settlement of Analco sit on level ground. The buried town is a flattened blueprint for the plaza, main alleys, and modern adobe architecture. It occupies the city's subconscious, molding its integrity and its fate. It teaches the streams of skiers and tourists patience. It reminds inhabitants to paint the doors and windows blue, respect the circle and the high wall, honor earth and water.

The city is an oasis, the end of the trail for Hispanic settlers and freedom-seeking American pioneers whose ghosts haunt the old adobe houses. The ancient hag who walked the canals of Tenochtitlán cries for her lost children along the banks of the Santa Fé River. St. Joseph, in the guise of an itinerant carpenter, came to build a miraculous staircase for the Sisters of Loretto. The message of St. Francis, harmonious with the Pueblo, encourages us to live as brothers and sisters to the sun, moon, and all earth's creatures. It is no accident that Santa Fé is a center for spiritual healing. The real city of Santa Fé, spreading above the Indian pueblo, that rests above prehistoric campsites, that rests above the antediluvian silt by the river, is as transitory and invisible.

The Indians selling jewelry under the portal of the Palace of the Governors are registered, certified, permit-wearing participants in the museum's living history exhibit. Day after day, snow or shine, they are the picture of longevity and cultural continuity. Instead of inlaid bone scrapers, they produce practical items like money clips, watch bands, key chains, sheaths for pen knives, and cigarette lighters in silver and turquoise, sometimes using commercial findings and factory-made stamps manufactured in Albuquerque. Alongside the souvenirs lie turquoise mosaic on red spondylus shell,

Zuñi jeweler Della Casi wearing a squash blossom necklace with clustered turquoise settings, a baroque style that developed in the 1920s. Photograph by Frasher.

strands of turquoise tabs, chunks, and disk-shaped beads, turquoise pendant earrings, and Jacla ear strings, which have been popular for at least a thousand years.

The jewelry traditional since the turn of this century displays astonishing technical skill: Zuñi bracelets in fine turquoise needlepoint, necklaces of Zuñi animal fetishes, and, from Santo Domingo, turquoise hishi polished so thin it is miraculous. The Hopis work in solid silver overlay, creating geometric designs, mythical serpents and flute players, vignettes of village life, and silhouettes of people driving trucks across the desert.

Perhaps the small figures are portraits of their makers, off to sell and have a good time at an Indian craft fair, Pow-Wow, or Feast Day. Perhaps they are on their way to buy supplies, meet a gem dealer, or hunt for turquoise. Jewelers, notoriously, never stop working.

They also are secretive about private sources. Major deposits are well-known, and turquoise from these commercial mines are distinguishable. Besides the stones from Mount Chalchihuitl near Cerrillos, prospectors have uncovered other prehistoric mines which still yield turquoise: Hachita and Orogrande in southern New Mexico, Leadville in Colorado, Mineral Park, Aztec Mountain, and the Dragoons in Arizona, Belmont in Nevada, and the Manvel mines outside Needles, California.

Ute warriors of the Kah-poh-teh band, northern New Mexico, model the full dress typical of Plains tribes. The spectacular braid of silver *conchas* shows the influence of Plains hair ornaments on the evolution of the Navajo *concha* belt. Daguerreotype by T. H. O'Sullivan, Wheeler Expedition of 1874.

Some people prefer the rich blue of Kingman, the green of Manassas, sky-blue Morenci, Bisbee black matrix, Sleeping Beauty, spider web and sea foam to flawless blue. Gem dealers now are importing quantities of deep blue turquoise from China. Mines deplete, new mines open, and tastes change. Itinerant merchants travel great distances to supply stones to Pueblo and Navajo craftspeople. Some jewelers take the time to search for turquoises, because it is cheaper and because they are looking for unique stones. A Zuñi woman and her husband know a place where turquoise lies near the surface in the Valley of Pines. "It's best to leave some stones growing in the ground and not dig them up too fast," she says. "The hardest and bluest stones are deeper. The longer you wait the better the stone."

The merits of a stone—its hardness, color, and luster—depend on whether it will be strung on a necklace or filed to fit silver channels or patterned inlays. In time the color of turquoise will change as the stone absorbs body oils, soap, and water. If turquoise is to dominate a ring or bracelet, the final criterion is how well the stone suits the setting.

Compared to the long history of turquoise jewelry in the Southwest, metalworking is relatively recent. Spanish settlers introduced ironsmithing and silver ornaments during the colonial period. A Mexican craftsman, wandering north in the nine-

teenth century, taught a Navajo blacksmith the rudiments of silversmithing and some basic designs. A Navajo smith, Atsidi Chon, set a solitary turquoise stone in a silver ring around 1880. The stone probably came from Cerrillos. Since then, Navajo rings, bracelets, and bow guards typically feature large stones and relatively heavy settings. The Zuñis, occupying a major turquoise trading center, had developed their refined lapidary skills over the centuries. The Pueblos of Santo Domingo controlled the Cerrillos mines and had ample quantities of turquoise for making beads. As soon as traders started providing better tools and silver, the Navajos and their Pueblo students were turning out polished pieces for distant buyers.

By 1920, traders had opened a tourist market for Indian jewelry and Fred Harvey, the railroad and hotel entrepreneur, was setting tastes. Beginning with stamped designs in imitation of Mexican leather work and floral decorative influences from the eastern United States, Southwestern jewelry styles grew to reflect broad international design movements such as Art Deco and Modern. Although a number of contemporary Indian jewelers are designing nontraditional pieces, the flare of their creations relies on superlative craftsmanship, mastery of traditional techniques like inlay, and original settings for traditional stones like picture jasper, lapis lazuli, coral, and turquoise.

The most coveted traditional ornaments today—the *concha* belt, squash blossom necklace, and *ketoh*—possess symbolic significance. The *concha* belt, as the name suggests, is made of silver shells. Indians, though extremely fond of shells, have never been known to string them around their waists. The belt is a grand adaptation of Spanish horse trappings. The Spaniards and the Greeks before them believed that turquoise protected horses and riders. The Navajo invention of the turquoise-studded *concha* belt raises coincidence to the realm of art and art to magic, encircling the hips in an expansive charm, preventing the rider from falling off his horse accidentally or sustaining any serious blow when he leaves the saddle.

The squash blossom necklace guarantees fertility. The silver squash blossom grew from a pomegranate, symbol of passion in the Old World. The design was borrowed from the Spanish, who borrowed it from the Moors. On traditional pieces, the hands reaching out at each end of the central blossom are sure signs of the symbol's Oriental derivation. In the New World the murals of Teotihuacán show odd little doglike creatures, with hands similarly posed, emerging from giant conch shells. The doglike creatures may be animated caricatures of the amorphous life forms that inhabit shells. The conch is the symbol of Quetzalcoatl. Eighth-century battle murals at Cacaxtla in central Mexico show an eagle warrior standing before the symbol of an open blue square closed by two hands clasping. The square arms are painted with Venus signs, symbol for war. The hands may represent peace. Southwestern jewelers say the hands of the squash blossom represent friendship.

The *ketoh*, or bow guard, was a wide leather strap that protected the archer's arm against the snap of the bowstring. Silversmiths took an interest in decorating the *ketoh* about the time when the bow and arrow fell out of use. *Ketohs* are now ceremonial. Early pieces were often sandcast. The most popular design represented the four directions. "When there are three or four openings, casting is easier. Filling the four corners may have developed because of sand casting," noted Navajo jeweler Yazzie Johnson in a recent exhibition. The *ketoh* is a perfect example of technique complementing symbol and purpose.

Stylized motifs stamped on silver have a simple and direct symbolic value. The cactus flower represents courtship, the rattlesnake jaw, strength, the broken arrow, peace. The Zia sun symbol, which stands for happiness, decorates not only jewelry but also every road sign in New Mexico. Hearts are expendable. The swastika, universal sign of good fortune, has assumed dark overtones. The wisdom of the "medicine man's eye" reaches to the Huichol area and all the way to faroff Zinacantán. The revival of ancient designs was inspired by traders

Shell with hands and dog head, Teotihuacán

and tourism. Ubiquity makes these symbols suspect, "touristy."

The thunderbird, although not indigenous to the Southwest, is prominent in Native American lore. Lord of storms, he sweeps down from northern Canada, soaring over the Great Lakes, the Northwest Coast, the yellow prairies, and the mountains of Mexico. The earth quakes and the sky turns black as he flies. His eyes flash lightning, his claws hurl lightning bolts. His closest relative is the monstrous Knife-Wing of the Zuñis. The Southwestern image of the thunderbird is based on a pictograph of a tamer bird. When the design became the trademark of the Santa Fé railroad, he began riding thundering locomotives across the plains. Fred Harvey encouraged Indian silversmiths to stamp the design on bracelets. Now the thunderbird circles the world on the arms of tourists.

Less conventional designs taken from petroglyphs are not yet commonplace. Their power depends on the craftsman's interpretation and execution. Deer, hummingbirds, butterflies, and plumed serpents, hero twins, kachinas, and the humpbacked flute player have complex mythical resonances, which link the Southwest to the larger Mesoamerican sphere. The simple stamp of a triangle emitting rays and called Morning Star is the sign of Tlaloc. Other abstract motifs which bear some resemblance to the Maya long-lipped god or

Peslakai Atsidi, "Slender Maker," in turquoise beaded necklaces, turquoise ear pendants, silver beads, and crescent pendant, the forerunner of the squash blossom necklace, holds a *concha* belt of plain silver disks strung on leather. His legendary brother, Atsidi Chon, was the first Navajo to have learned silverworking from Mexican craftsmen. Photograph by Ben Wittick, c. 1885.

to the Olmec jaguar's U-shaped brow are too faint to suggest a positive derivation.

Some collectors scoff at the influence of outsiders on Native American crafts. The techniques developed with the help of white traders are too refined to be attributed simply to tourism. The encouragement to resurrect and adapt old designs sparked a true native revival. This book draws parallels between Southwestern and Mexican cultures. Many influences came from the land to the south. Perhaps the common myths and motifs originated sometime in the dim past with the people of the Southwest, were carried in the mind, and were evoked thousands of years later. Certainly the Pueblo and Navajo silversmiths have made them their own.

Art conveys symbols that travel through history. The earth has its patterns, too. Lapidaries are fond of saying that they are simply freeing the forms and patterns hidden in the stone. Objects of beauty and mystery become treasures because they possess the power of the thing represented and the power of earthly material. In craft, the line between nature and artifice dissolves.

Old turquoise necklaces are preserved as heirlooms worn only on ritual occasions. Ancient Native Americans often "killed" ritual objects once their sacred purpose was fulfilled, returning them, like once living things, to the earth, where they were visible only to the gods. The earth buried them further, until someone with trained eyes was able to discern signs in the landscape. The earth has a mind of its own, just as time has a mind of its own. There is a conspiracy between earth, rocks, and trees, hiding and then revealing through natural clues the shapes of fallen cities, the spot of buried treasure, and pieces of history and culture.

The American past is a series of abandoned rooms. New residents move in, inventing stories of the previous occupants, praising or desecrating the things left behind. When Europeans began moving west, the cities and pyramids of the Mound Builders were empty. The Hohokam, Mogollon, and Anasazi cultures of the Southwest had disappeared, because irrigation eventually poisoned the soil. The civilization of the romantic American West, with its dams, overgrazing, and stripmining, may suffer a similar fate. Sooner or later, the Turquoise Land may heal and make a home.

Follow a stone and discover an endless story, beginning with ten-thousand-year-old footprints in the mud. The trail is the ceremonial road at Cobá and the ceremonial road at Chaco Canyon. The trail links Mixtec goldsmiths, Tarascan coppersmiths, and Navajo silversmiths. The trail is the Hopi journey of life and the steps of Quetzalcoatl, the man with footsteps of wind.

SELECTED BIBLIOGRAPHY

CHAPTER 1

Folsom, Franklin. *The Life and Legend of George McJunkin, Black Cowboy*. New York: Lodestar Books, 1973.

Stanford, Dennis F., and Jane Day, eds. *Ice Age Hunters of the Rockies*. Denver: Denver Museum of Natural History and University Press of Colorado, 1992.

Waters, Frank. *Book of the Hopi*. New York: Penguin Books, 1963.

Wormington, Marie M. *Ancient Man in North America*. Denver: Denver Museum of Natural History, 1957.

CHAPTER 2

Benson, Elizabeth P., ed. *The Olmec and their Neighbors: Essays in Memory of Matthew Sterling*. Washington, D.C.: Dumbarton Oaks, 1981.

Caso, Alfonso. *Reyes y reinos de la Mixteca*. Mexico: Fondo de Cultura Economica, 1977.

Coe, Michael. *Mexico*. New York: Frederick A. Praeger, 1969.

———. "Olmec Jaguars and Olmec Kings" in *The Cult of the Feline*, edited by Elizabeth P. Benson. Washington, D.C.: Dumbarton Oaks, 1972.

DiPeso, Charles C. "Archaeology and Ethnohistory of the Northern Sierra," in *Handbook of Middle American Indians*, Vol. 4, Archaeological Frontiers and External Connections, Gordon F. Ekholm and Gordon R. Willey, eds., Robert Wauchope, gen. ed. Austin: University of Texas Press, 1978.

Foster, Michael, and Phil C. Weigand. *The Archeology of West and Northwest Mesoamerica*. Boulder: Westview Press, 1986.

Galeano, Eduardo. *Memory of Fire*, Part 1, *Genesis*, Cedric Belfrage, trans. New York: Pantheon, 1985.

Hammond, Norman. *Ancient Maya Civilization*. New Brunswick: Rutgers University Press, 1982.

Harbottle, Garman, and Phil C. Weigand. "The Mining and Trade for Turquoise in Ancient Mesoamerica," in *Scientific American*, 1992.

Holien, Thomas. *Mesoamerican Pseudo-Cloisonné and Other Decorative Investments*. PhD dissertation. Carbondale: University of Southern Illinois, 1977.

Jurnigan, E. Wesley. *Jewelry of the Prehistoric Southwest*. Santa Fe, Albuquerque: School of American Research and University of New Mexico Press,1978.

Kelley, J. Charles. "Mesoamerica and the Southwestern United States," in *Handbook of Middle American Indians*, Vol.4, Archaeological Frontiers and External Connections, Gordon F. Ekholm and Gordon R. Willey, eds., Robert Wauchope, gen. ed. Austin: University of Texas Press, 1978.

Lee, Thomas A., and Carlos Navarrette. *Mesoamerican Communication Routes and Cultural Contacts*. Papers of the New World Archeological Foundation, No. 40. Provo: Brigham Young University, 1978.

Mathien, F. and R. McGuire. *Ripples in the Chichimec Sea*. Carbondale: Southern Illinois University Press, 1986.

Miller, Arthur G., *The Mural Painting of Teotihuacàn*. Washington, D.C.: Dumbarton Oaks, 1973.

Morris, Ann Axtell. "The Hidden Turquoise Mosaic," in *Conquistadors Without Swords: Archeologists in the Americas*, edited by Leo Deuel. New York: Schocken,1974.

Riley, L. Carroll and Basil Hedrick, eds. *Across the Chichimec Sea*. Carbondale: Southern Illinois University Press, 1978.

Frog, Mimbres

Rothenberg, Jerome. *Shaking the Pumpkin: Traditional Poetry of the Indian North Americas*. Garden City, N.Y.: Doubleday, 1972.

Sahagún, Fray Bernadino de. *General History of the Things of New Spain*, Arthur J.O. Anderson and Charles E. Dibble, trans. Santa Fe: School of American Research, 1961.

Schele, Linda, and David Freidel. *A Forest of Kings: The Untold Story of the Ancient Maya*. New York: William Morrow and Co., 1990.

Schaafsma, Polly, and Curtis Schaafsma. "Evidence for the Origins of the Pueblo Katchina Cult as Suggested by Southwestern Rock Art," in *American Antiquity*, 39, 1974.

Stephens, John Lloyd. *Incidents of Travel in Central America, Chiapas and Yucatan*. New York: Harper and Brothers, 1841.

Thompson, Marc. "Codes of the Underworld: Mimbres Iconography Revealed." Paper Presented at the 6th Annual Mogollon Conference, October, 1990, Western New Mexico University, Silver City, New Mexico.

Weigand, Phil C., Garman Harbottle, and Edward V. Sayre. "Turquoise Sources and Source Analysis: Mesoamerica and the Southwestern U.S.A." in *Exchange Systems in Prehistory*, Timothy Earle and J. Ericson, eds.. New York: Academic Press, 1977.

Weigand, Phil C., and Garman Harbottle. "The Role of Turquoises in the Ancient Mesoamerican Trade Structure" in *Prehistoric Exchange Systems in North America*, J. E. Ericson and T. G. Baugh, eds. New York: Plenum Press.

Whitecotton, Joseph W., *The Zapotecs: Princes, Priests, and Peasants*. Norman: University of Oklahoma Press, 1977.

CHAPTER 3

Between Sacred Mountains: Navajo Stories and Lessons from the Land, vol.11. Foreword by N. Scott Momaday. Tucson: Sun Tracks and the University of Arizona Press, Tucson, 1982.

Galeano, Eduardo. *Memory of Fire*, Part 1, *Genesis*, Cedric Belfrage, trans. New York: Pantheon Books, 1985.

Cushing, Frank Hamilton. *Zuni, Selected Writings*, Jesse Green, ed. Lincoln: University of Nebraska Press, 1979.
_____. *Zuñi Fetishes*. Facsimile Edition. Las Vegas: KC Publications, 1988.

Karasik, Carol, ed. *People of the Bat: Tales and Dreams from Zinacantan*, collected and trans. by Robert M. Laughlin. Washington, D.C.: Smithsonian Institution Press, 1988.

Lincoln, Kenneth. *Native American Renaissance*. Berkeley: University of California Press, 1983.

Ortiz, Alfonso. *The Tewa World: Space, Time, Being and Becoming in a Pueblo Society*. Chicago: Universiy of Chicago Press, 1969.

Parsons, Elsie C. *Pueblo Indian Religion*. Chicago: University of Chicago Press, 1939.

Pogue, Joseph E. *The Turquois*. Washington, D.C.: National Academy of Sciences, 1915.

Rothenberg, Jerome. *Shaking the Pumpkin: Traditional Poetry of the Indian North Americas*. Garden City, N.Y.: Doubleday, 1972.

Schaafsma, Polly. *Indian Rock Art of the Southwest*. Santa Fe: School of American Research and University of New Mexico Press, Albuquerque, 1980.

Tedlock, Dennis. *Popol Vuh, the Definitive Edition of the Mayan Book of the Dawn of Life and the Glories of Gods and Kings*. New York: Simon and Schuster, 1985.

Tyler, Hamilton A. *Pueblo Gods and Myths*. Norman: University of Oklahoma Press, 1964.

Underhill, Ruth Murray. *Singing for Power*. Berkeley: University of California Press, 1938.

CHAPTER 4

Babcock, William H. *Legendary Islands of the Atlantic: A Study in Medieval Geography*. American Geographical Society, Research Series No. 8. New York: American Geographical Society, 1925.

Cabeza de Vaca's Adventures in the Unknown Interior of America, Cyclone Covey, ed. and trans. Albuquerque: University of New Mexico Press, 1990.

Diaz del Castillo, Bernal. *Cortez and the Conquest of Mexico by the Spaniards in 1521*. Rep. of 1942 ed. Hamden, Ct.: Shoe String, 1988.

Irreverent comedians of the high and low, *Kossa* clowns joke in a language no one understands, steal food, steal the limelight, and in the dense heat of summer keep the dance in order. Photographed by T. Harmon Parkhurst at San Juan Pueblo, c. 1940.

Durán, Diego. *History of New Spain*. Norman: University of Oklahoma Press, 1971.

Galeano, Eduardo. *Memory of Fire: Century of the Wind, Vol. III*. Cedric Belfrage, trans. New York: Pantheon, 1988.

Hammond, George P., and Agapito Rey. *Coronado Cuarto Centennial Publications, 1540-1940*; Vol. 2, *Narratives of the Coronado Expedition, 1540-1542*. Albuquerque: University of New Mexico Press, 1940.

_____. Vol 5, *Don Juan de Oñate, Colonizer of New Mexico, 1595–1628*. Albuquerque: University of New Mexico Press, 1953.

Martyr, Peter (Pietro Martire D'Anghiera). "The Golden World," in *The Portable Renaissance Reader*, James Bruce Ross and Mary Martin McLaughlin, eds. New York: Penguin, 1977.

Northrup, Stuart A. *Turquoise and Spanish Mines in New Mexico*. Albuquerque: University of New Mexico Press, 1975.

Parry, John H. *The Age of Reconnaissance*. Cleveland: World Books, 1963.

Portilla-Léon, Miguel, ed. *The Broken Spears: The Aztec Account of the Conquest of Mexico*, Lysander Kemp, trans. Boston: Beacon Press, 1972.

Riley, Carroll L. "The Road to Hawikuh: Trade and Trade Routes to Cibola-Zuñi During Late Prehistoric and Early Historic Times," in *The Kiva*, Vol. 41, No. 2, 1975.

Sahagún, Fray Bernadino de. *General History of the Things of New Spain*, Arthur J. O. Anderson and Charles E. Dibble, trans. Santa Fe: School of American Research, 1961.

Sayer, Chloe. *The Arts and Crafts of Mexico*. San Francisco: Chronicle, 1990.

Spicer, Edward W. *Cycles of Conquest: The Impact of Spain, Mexico and the United States on the Indians of the Southwest, 1553-1960*. Tucson: University of Arizona Press, 1962.

Water, Frank. *Masked Gods: Navaho and Pueblo Ceremonialism*. Athens, Ohio: Swallow Press, 1950.

CHAPTER 5

Adair, John. *The Navajo and Pueblo Silversmiths*. Norman: University of Oklahoma Press, 1944.

Gage, Thomas. *Thomas Gage's Travels in the New World*, J. Eric S. Thompson, ed. Norman: University of Oklahoma Press, 1969.

ACKNOWLEDGMENTS

Trails never end, but books do. I want to thank my editor, Beverly Fazio, for her trust and patience from the beginning to the whirlwind finale. Nancy Schandelmeier, Dinah Wiley, Susanna Ekholm, Ambar Past, and Glenn Shepard improved drafts of my manuscript.

I am indebted to the scholars who blazed the trail, especially Phil Weigand, who headed me in the right direction; Curtis Schaafsma, who armed me with the basics in Southwestern archaeology, and the adventure; and Alfonso Ortiz, who appeared at different places on the trail to remind me of the truth beyond facts. Others shared their knowledge and insights and put up with my endless questions: Peter Jimenez Betts; Linda Schele; Tom Chavez; Charles Bennett; Richard Rudisill; Joan Mathien; Louise Stiver; Bettina Raphael; Artie Yellowhorse; Mark Arrowsmith; Charlie Bird; and Alma King of Santa Fe East.

Many explorers, artists, and wanderers have guided me on my journey. I honor the memory of painter Alfred Jensen who set me on the path of the ancient Maya. I am grateful to friends who have offered limitless kindness, encouragement, and waystations on the road: my *maestros* Travis Hartley and David Haun, who taught me all I know about gemstones, bending silver, and the jeweler's art; Chip Morris, textile trader and living legend, for a helping hand on the high road and the low; Marcey Jacobson and Janet Marren for leading the way; Susanna Ekholm for huge helpings of archaeological knowledge and dirt, rum and sympathy; Ambar Past, for poetry, hotels, books, paper, chocolate, treehouse, woods, rain or shine; Alfred Bush for generously allowing me to read and dream in Sapos Santos; Jane Taylor; Frances Méndez; Gabriel and Kiki Suarez; Kevin Gruark; and Glenn Shepard, who kept me dancing; in Santa Fé, Peter and Suzanne Ruta, Judy Margolis, and Judith Roberts, I can say no more; John Burstein, who saved me time and again; Ray and Nancy Schandelmeier, whose kitchen is the center of the world; Dinah and Foster Wiley, who showed the love of true warriors; Kristi Butterwick for trips through the desert and drawers of museums; Andrea Baltman, my sister on the highway of life; and Roger Snodgrass, with whom I shared countless adventures in Mexico and the Southwest, discovering where all ladders start.

Robert Laughlin taught me that the genius of anthropology lies in the heart. Mimi Laughlin shared her home and magic garden, and saw me through. My life and work would be impossible without the faith of my aunt, Rebecca Cole, and my step-mother, Edna.

This book is dedicated to my father, Frank Karasik, to whom I owe my slow steps, distant sights, and my art.

—C.K.

This book is dedicated to my friendship with Jeff and Cheryl Weisberg—friends indeed. Also, to my first "ethnographic" subjects, Joseph (Tonkas) McEwan and his wife, Elvira, both resourceful peasant farmers who lived and died in the Blue Mountains of Jamaica. I wanted to grow old with them.

Jeffrey Lewis lives the story of the turquoise trade route. In the 60s he traveled to the rain forest of Mexico at the behest of Hopi shamen to secure protection at the source of sacred feathers. His understanding and trust gave my work a great boost. Bettina Raphael opened doors to museums where access was critical. Nancy Dahl and Dan Murphy shared friendship, knowledge, opinions, and connections.

Many people helped me on the trail. I'm honored to name them here: Jean Mead, who put a key under a rock by her front door; Ben Barney, who offered an unedited view of Navajo life; John Burstein, a shock absorber on the trail; Cheryl Fairbanks and Regis Pecos; Verna Williamson; Linna and Duke Davis, pathfinders to some of my best experiences; Tom Woodard, who shared his wit and fine jewelry; Joe Tanner; Frank Starks and Carolyn Bobelu, who showed me beautiful jewelry and hospitality; Lane Coutler; David (Desert Lobo) Leonard, who took me on the "Journado de Muerto"; Carl Hartman, who gave me shelter from the cold; Rex and Mark Arrowsmith, both generous and knowledgeable; Bill Malone, Hubbell Trading Post; Don Owen, SWAIA; Nita Davis of Ramah; Sharon Maloof; Chester and Dorothy Mahooty; Robin & Ringo; Jim Ostler and Milford Nahohai, Pueblo of Zuni Arts and Crafts Cooperative; the Pickelner brothers, Steve and David; Marsha Bol, Museum of International Folk Art; Eunice Kahn, Steve Rogers, and Linette Miller, Wheelwright Museum; Cathey Billian; Terry Walpole and Susanne Ahmann; Harvey Lloyd and Shirley Price; Gary Avey and Margret Clark-Price, *Native Peoples Magazine*; Jack Parsons; Arlyn Shakya, Zuni guide; Lynn Britner, School of American Research; Louise Stiver, Lab of Anthropology; Lloyd Oxendine; Babette Bloch; Erica Benowitz; Idel Conaway; Audry Supple; and the Westside Color Lab/NYC.

The home team remains steadfast. They are Christiana Dittmann (in a class by herself), Philip H. Foxx, A. J. Saunders, Phil Cantor, Larry LaBonte and Kathy Shaw, Garry Gross, Izzy and Crystal Seidman, Richard Campagna, Roger Rosen, and Atsuko Ikeda.

My thanks as well to the talented people at Abrams who gave this project its form: Beverly Fazio, Sam Antupit, Maria Miller, Liz Robbins, and Nanice Lund. Very special thanks to Marti Malovany.

—J.J.F.